Union Public Library

P9-CEA-793

DOÑA TOMÁS

DOÑA TOMÁS

DISCOVERING AUTHENTIC MEXICAN COOKING

THOMAS SCHNETZ AND DONA SAVITSKY
WITH MIKE WILLE

Union Public Library

FOREWORD BY RICHARD RODRIGUEZ

PHOTOGRAPHY BY ED ANDERSON

TEN SPEED PRESS
BERKELEY / TORONTO

Copyright © 2006 by Thomas Schnetz and Dona Savitsky
Photographs © 2006 by Ed Anderson
Foreword © 2006 by Richard Rodriguez

All rights reserved. No part of this book may be reproduced in any form, except brief excerpts
for the purpose of review, without written permission of the publisher.

Ten Speed Press
Box 7123
Berkeley, California 94707
www.tenspeed.com

Distributed in Australia by Simon and Schuster Australia, in Canada by Ten Speed Press
Canada, in New Zealand by Southern Publishers Group, in South Africa by Real Books, and in
the United Kingdom and Europe by Publishers Group UK.

Cover and text design by Ed Anderson / Skout

Library of Congress Cataloging-in-Publication Data on file with publisher.

Printed in China

2 3 4 5 6 7 8 9 10 – 11 10 09 08 07

CONTENTS

FOREWORD

This is a book of recipes from Doña Tomás restaurant, where there are long lines every night, even if you come, as I most often do, at five-thirty. The success of Doña Tomás (located on the border between Berkeley and Oakland), I propose, is not its recovery of "authentic" Mexican. I think its popularity represents a final and glorious triumph of the bastard!

Diana Kennedy, the holy mother of authentic Mexican cuisine, relentlessly cautions her readers: Mexican cooking is an entirely different matter from Mexican American food. Indeed. When I was growing up, I wondered why food at Mexican American restaurants was so bloated, so un-spontaneous, so corny, so tepid—"hot plates"—nothing at all like the Mexican food of my home. The gringo apparently sought something recognizably, dependably foreign—a formula. In time, through church bazaars, school bazaars, and potlucks, most Californians began to distinguish between home recipes and clichés.

In its August 2004 obituary for Julia Child, the *New York Times* noted that Child "admitted she could live without" Mexican food. Well, rest in peace. Who knows how many Mexican American restaurants in Boston or Santa Barbara tutored Ms. Child's prejudice.

Diana Kennedy, though celebrated, is less famous than Ms. Child, but she is, to my taste, the more interesting example of the expatriate-explorer-interpreter. Julia Child was the American who traveled to Europe. She returned to teach her fellow Americans not to fear the heights of French cooking. The rules were many, but simple enough in sequence.

Diana Kennedy is the European who discovered the Americas (for our purposes, the more interesting journey). She arrived in Mexico from England in the late 1950s and was immediately seduced by a vibrant cuisine. In the decades that followed, she set about unraveling its spices, scents, and colors to become an anthropologist of sorts—the principal excavator of pre-Columbian and colonial recipes. It is Kennedy's conviction that the cooking of peasant and indigenous Mexico is in fact a classic cuisine.

My nephew, Tom Schnetz (the "Tomás" of Doña Tomás), admits to me that his first love was France. Tom did not grow up in a storybook Mexican kitchen or in a family of magical-realist confectioners. My father, Tom's grandfather, was inventive and dexterous—even happy—in the kitchen, but plain in his tastes—eggs, beans, onions, chorizo. My mother's favorite supper was a plate of beans my father had cooked and a loaf of good French bread. Tom's mother is a straightforwardly American cook.

After college, Tom went to Paris and he lived there for a time. Just to see. I admire him for that. He returned from Paris looking like a French poster of himself: very Ernesto, very Pablo. In his French recovery period, Tom dreamed up a cliché—of someday opening a French country inn in some glamorous cleft of the Sonoma hills. Luckily for Tom, luckily for us, he met the woman who became his coconspirator in matters of food, Dona Savitsky. Dona trained his appetite southward.

Dona is not Mexican; Tom is German on his father's side. Their restaurant's success is a brown, saucy story. For brown is the true banner of Mexico, and all who live under the influence of Mexico swim in the sauce of mixed metaphor. The notorious erotic appetite of Mexico (its temptation to the gringo, but also perhaps its fearsomeness for the gringo) is its capacity to pour, to cross, to violate exact instructions, to blend and stir and spill a little, and see what happens. But also to receive. To open its blanket to morels or oysters or radishes or cream or haricots verts or brandy.

That a British woman, Mrs. Kennedy, should attempt to codify Mexico's recipes—which are one might almost say the passing humor of indigenous Mexican villages—is a fine Mexican irony. It is she who tells her American readers of the blending of Olmec, Maya, and Aztec traditions on a plate and how those tastes merged within the Spanish conquests. That last fold—the *mestizaje*—marrying Indian and Spaniard, is the great recipe of Mexico, from which all other recipes descend; from which Doña Tomás descends. The birth of the bastard.

Octavio Paz, the conscience and writer of Mexico's last century, remarked on the enormous psychological border separating Mexico from the United States, not least in the kitchen: "Traditional North American cooking is a cuisine with no mysteries: simple, spiceless, nutritious food. No tricks: The carrot is an honest carrot, the potato is not ashamed of being a potato."

Paz calls this the "Puritan impulse" within American culture—our disinclination to live with mixture and the Yankee preference for black and white. Paz observes how remote American recipes are, how standoffish the portions on the plate—the vegetables drawing away from the cadaver. How different from the murky and muddy Mexican swamps—"green, red, and yellow sauces . . . a major scandal."

To this day, the puritans try to straighten our American appetite. Obesity!—their latest outcry. The puritans at the Center for Science in the Public Interest in Washington have regularly warned consumers against such dietary dangers as chow mein and pizza. Trans fat is the very devil. So, also, beware, beware, combination plate #3: the chile relleno is "the equivalent of eating a full cube of butter."

Sociologists tell us of the relationship between Protestantism and capitalism. The former gave rise to the latter. But somehow the latter hijacked the former. Capitalism, for example, took the simple, the good carrot, refined and bleached it of taste and nutrition, dyed it orange, boiled it in sucrose, and canned it.

The revolutionary innovation (truly a restoration) in California in recent years, personified by Alice Waters at Chez Panisse restaurant, was to recover the simple carrot—to grow it in the restaurant's own garden, to rescue it from wicked, wrong-headed processing. Chez Panisse thus represents some interesting marriage of Julia Child's buttery Catholic France with whole-grain Puritan Berkeley, both subsumed under the ancient folkway: eat what is fresh and seasonal.

Tex-Mex is preferable, to my mind, to Cal-Mex—the two competitors for the American appetite. The former is hot-breathed, spicy, and ragged, reflecting the violent struggle between the Mexican and the so-called "Anglo" in Texas. It is a cowboy cuisine—a daredevil duel, a boast.

And yet, if you go to a "Mexican" restaurant in Sydney or in Tokyo or that awful one in Times Square, and even, yes, even in Paris (I found three within a short walk from my hotel recently), you are likely to find Cal-Mex, not Tex. Perhaps this is only a result of the power of Los Angeles on the world's imagination—its theatrical reach—or represents some standardization. The bad Mexican restaurant, like the bad Chinese or the bad Italian restaurant, cooks for the client's expectation and does not exceed it.

Doña Tomás is Cal-Mex of a sort we have never tasted. It rejects the blandness of California Mexican cooking, but also the greasy bathos of it. Doña Tomás belongs to the nouvelle California initiative for the pure and the good. It is fresh cooking; it is Protestant cooking. But it is cooking plainly in love with the South, with lavishness and arousal, arabesque and surprise. This is cooking that works against expectation. Therein lies its Mexican authenticity.

And I said to Tom, who was brooding over the crustiness of a huge square pan of—what? Bread pudding? Look, Tom, you have got to tell me how to end this thing, otherwise, I will write in circles till the cows come home. And Tom said, No, it's good enough, just stop.

—RICHARD RODRIGUEZ

GRACIAS

THOMAS SCHNETZ

I would like to dedicate this book to the following people:

To Dona, for mixing business and friendship, a better partner I could not have hoped for.

To Mike Wille, for having the true talent of putting pen to paper and somehow making our cryptic recipes become legible.

To Phil Wood, for eating our food from the very start.

To my chefs and cooks—Juan Zarate, Matthew Ridgeway, Lucio Alvarado, Martin Matias, Jose Alvarado, Eva Gomez, Jose Luis Aguilar, Hilda Rodriguez, Jose Gomez, Jose Juan Rodriguez, and Eduardo Rodriguez. I am very proud of both kitchens.

To Genni Combes, Shiela Ennis, Danny Rimer, and Jon Underwood, for helping us in the beginning when we needed it most.

To Jim Pettit, our patron, for being a great friend to the restaurant and to us personally.

To Ed Anderson, for creating photographs that can stand alone in their beauty.

To Carrie Rodrigues and Clancy Drake, our editors, for overseeing this project and making it come to life.

To Paul Buscemi, Loretta Keller, and Gary Woo, for sharing their knowledge and teaching me how to cook, and my friend Jennifer Millar, for passing along many a dessert recipe.

To my uncle Richard Rodriguez and my aunt Mary Schnetz, for generously helping out over the years and to my mother-in-law, Moira Moniz, for letting us max out her credit cards.

To my family—my dad, Earl; my mom, Sylvia; my brother, David; and my sister, Christine—for helping build, finance, and decorate while still letting me remain in the family.

To Jackson, who helped me build Doña Tomás, oftentimes strapped to my chest in a baby carrier or helping me hammer nails into the walls.

To Ethan, who attended his share of planning meetings for Tacubaya and helped inspect the construction, often with his lightsaber in hand.

To my wife, Anjeannette, for helping me live my dreams. I love you with all my heart.

DONA SAVITSKY

To Tom, my "restaurant husband"; I am very thankful that he is willing to do the things I dislike. For his great style and flair that ring throughout our restaurants, making them beautiful, and for sharing a vision that we can always do things our way and consistently do them well. Most of all, I would like to thank Tom for believing we can balance a successful restaurant with our own fulfilling family lives, and reassuring me of this whenever I get overwhelmed.

To Tom, my "domestic husband," who is not intimidated by my success but encourages me to achieve my goals. He has been a continuous source of inspiration because of his vision, optimism, and faith in my talents. For all the long nights of Sheetrocking, tiling, and painting that he poured into Doña Tomás while our children were asleep on the floor. For grounding me when I may have freaked out and for filling in as a bartender or host without notice or experience, but most of all, for taking risks and being proud of me.

To Andee, my right-hand woman whose tireless dedication and assistance help us run our restaurants. For all of the propane tank filling, errand running, no-show-waiter-filling-in, and broken wheel repairing, not to mention the outfit emergencies and blistered feet from working in high heels . . . she has been a true gift and a very special friend and confidante.

To my three kids—Dylan, Zora, and Ella—for always bringing me back to earth and reminding me that work is good but love is better. I am very lucky to have them in my life.

To my original family—mom, dad, and sister: thanks for making me the woman I am.

To all the staff at both restaurants, every day I feel extremely fortunate to work with each and every one of them: Aimee, Angy, Brandon, Brian, Carlos, Christopher, Claudio, Enrique, Hannah, Heather, Isaias, Itzel, Jesus, Jose O., Jose Sr., Jose Luis, Josef, Juan Jr., Julia, Kara, Karol, Luis, Luke, Lynne, Oracio, Paul, Rigoberto, Robert, Sahar, Sally, Salvador, and Tommy.

To Louise Clement, Julia Drori, Donna Sieff, Maria Chavez, Joyce Goldstein, Diana Kennedy, and all the other kick-ass women I have had the good fortune of rubbing elbows with.

To Denny Abrams and all the folks at Abrams/Millikan, for helping with the birth of Tacubaya. And finally to all the other special people in my life who have made a difference in who I am—they all know who they are!

MIKE WILLE

I would like to thank Tom Schnetz, Dona Savitsky, and their staff for introducing me to their world of Mexican cuisine; the holy trinity of dried peppers; the three sisters of the Native Americans (corn, beans, and squash); the fresh California ingredients; and, of course, combination plate #3. This introduction involved endless hours of practice, research, ingredient scouting, and recipe testing, all of which yielded an invaluable harvest of new friendships and enlightening knowledge. It also provided my unborn son, Séamus, with a gestation diet of chiles, masa, and *frijoles*, until his mother could stand no more.

I would also like to thank the trinity of my immediate family—my wife, my mother, and my sister—three women who have provided me with more love and support than any one man could possibly ask for. And while I am speaking in the tongues of threes, I would like to thank all of my family and friends and the professional acquaintances who have been important parts of my life. The more our relationships grow, the less definitive the classifications become, enriching my life and my work.

INTRODUCTIONS

THOMAS SCHNETZ

Dona and I met in the kitchen of San Francisco's Square One in 1992. She had recently graduated from culinary school at Santa Barbara City College and I was a few years removed from a political science degree at U.C. Berkeley. We became fast friends (my wife and I even sharing a room with her then two-year-old son, Dylan, for a few months) and talked of someday opening a hotel and restaurant in Sonoma. We both moved on, Dona becoming chef at Café Marimba, while I worked at Bizou in San Francisco and also at a café that I opened with my brother in Sacramento called Marshall Grounds.

It wasn't until my wife and I moved back to Berkeley that our plans started to solidify. A house around the corner from us became available and Dona and her family moved in. If I may add something, Dona is married to Tom, and while my name is Tom, Dona and I are married in a business sense only. Furthermore, it just so happens that Dona's Tom possesses the surname Moniz, which also happens to be my wife Anjeannette's maiden name. And although my wife and Dona's husband share the same last name, they're not related either.

As our ideas evolved, opening a Mexican restaurant in Oakland made a lot of sense to us. We found a spot at 5004 Telegraph Avenue in the Temescal District, and on September 15, 1999 (the eve of Mexico's Independence Day), Doña Tomás was born. (Please note that we fully understand—and it has been pointed out on countless occasions—that the restaurant's name is incorrect Spanish. However, Dona's name is Dona and my name is Thomas, hence, the name Doña Tomás. My grandparents forgave me, so I hope others can too.)

At Doña Tomás we have tried to create food that is authentic to Mexico. There are no burritos or nachos in sight. We have committed ourselves to serving such household favorites as *chilaquiles* and

fideo as well as celebratory dishes like *chiles rellenos en nogada* and *pollo con mole coloradito*. We search out the best purveyors for our ingredients, using Niman Ranch meats for our carnitas and carne asada, Hoffman Gamebirds for chicken and quail, the Fresh Fish Company for local and seasonal fish, and Mayordomo in Oaxaca for chocolate. We have Greenleaf Produce to thank for procuring essential ingredients such as epazote, *verdolagas*, and *hoja santa* from local farmers. We have also been lucky enough to stumble upon a serendipitous supply of avocado leaves. At my new house, I would often find avocado pits on my lawn, and I couldn't figure out why my boys might be throwing them there. It was not until I spied a squirrel in one particular tree and, soon after, an avocado flying through the air, that I put the two together.

And of course, no Mexican meal would be complete without tortillas, which we hand-make with fresh masa from our favorite tortillerías, La Palma and La Finca. I realize that some chefs insist on slaking the lime and grinding their own corn, but masa is like bread; it is an integral part of the meal that often ends up being the most difficult component to produce consistently. We leave the masa-making to those who dedicate their lives to mastering the craft, while we focus simply on cooking and serving Mexican cuisine.

In July of 2003, Dona and I opened our version of a taquería at 1788 Fourth Street in Berkeley. We named it Tacubaya after a neighborhood in Mexico City in which the famed architect Luis Barragán lived. Much like Barragán's modern architecture, which in its purity and simplicity was respectful of tradition, we wanted to create a taquería that paid respect to traditional dishes such as *sopa de tortilla*, *tacos al pastor*, and *tamales con verduras*. Tacubaya has allowed us to re-create beloved dishes usually found in home kitchens, street vendor stands, and family taquerías.

Given that our last names are Savitsky and Schnetz, we are not immune to questions about the appropriateness of our serving the foods of Mexico. But Mexican food is in our blood. When Dona was chef at Café Marimba, she made some of the best regional Mexican food in the Bay Area. As for me, my grandparents on my mother's side came to California by way of Guadalajara and Minatitlán. Running Doña Tomás has given me a chance to partake in a part of Mexico that they left behind—its cuisine.

We have divided the recipes in this book into chapters on breakfast, lunch, salads and sides, and dinner, but the beauty of this food is that most of it can be eaten at any time of the day. We have included many of our favorite recipes (except the one for carnitas—everyone must have their secrets). Enjoy.

DONA SAVITSKY

As Tom and I were juggling the mind-boggling tasks required to open our first restaurant, one of the largest hurdles we encountered was trying to obtain a liquor license. For a brief moment we considered opening the doors without it, but I knew the dining experience would be incomplete without savoring a *sangría sandía* with our fresh ceviche, enjoying an icy margarita with our carnitas, or simply sipping a Michelada with our salty chips and smoky *pasilla de Oaxaca* salsa. After plenty of paperwork and a little knavery (we actually lost quite a bit of money trying to buy a license from a broker in L.A. who was selling revoked licenses), we finally landed the license and opened our doors in September 1999 in true celebratory style. Our party was definitely not dry.

Since Tom and I both have culinary backgrounds without a lot of bartending experience, neither of us ventured to the backside of the bar except to retrieve staff drinks. But we both knew how to balance flavors and we knew what we liked. So during the many evenings prior to our September opening, we did quite a bit of drink recipe testing. After plenty of trial runs and a few arduous hangovers, we finally came up with a list of drinks we feel reflects the philosophy of our concept while still holding true to Mexico's traditional cuisine.

Before we opened Tacubaya, we took a pilgrimage down to Southern California to visit as many taquerías as we could, indulging in the cuisines and absorbing the many different atmospheres. Although the food at most of these establishments was top-notch, with fresh masas, toasted chiles, and roasted tomatoes, most of them fell short when it came to their margaritas or aguas frescas, relying on powdered packets or concentrates and bottom-shelf spirits.

What we decided to serve at our restaurants, and what we have included in the book, are alcoholic and nonalcoholic drinks calling for fresh fruit, such as limes and watermelons, and traditional Mexican spices, such as canela and *piloncillo*. Many of our cocktails are riffs on old classics that have been modified to fit our style and can be adjusted any which way; just be certain to use quality liquors, such as 100 percent blue agave tequilas, to get the best flavor from your drinks.

AUTHORS' NOTE

Throughout this book, the pronoun "I" refers to Tom.

BÁSICOS

BASICS

INGREDIENTS - EQUIPMENT - TECHNIQUES

INGREDIENTS

Globalization has had profound effects on cultures and cuisines in both negative and positive respects. Some aspects of our lives develop at such a rapid pace that important methods, recipes, and pieces of tradition escape us and fall through the cracks of yesterday, only to remain as folklore and stories. In other ways, we gain a better understanding of our culture with technology guiding our research, uncovering what was once important, helping us marry yesterday's culinary traditions to modern-day cuisine.

At Doña Tomás and Tacubaya, we work hard to respect Mexico's culture while applying modern practices to ancient traditions. The availability of our fresh California ingredients, our urban setting and lifestyles, and the development of our own palates help define the direction of the food at both restaurants.

We find ourselves at a serendipitous point in culinary history, especially here in Berkeley and Oakland, where ingredients such as spices, dried chiles, and *piloncillo* sugar cones from thousands of miles away are sold at reasonable prices and can be shipped right to our front door. At the same time, our backyard is filled with the freshest of produce, fish, meat, and poultry.

I am not one of those chefs who grew up picking fresh blackberries with his parents during summer afternoon picnics, or eating tomatoes fresh out of Mom's garden sprinkled with sea salt and home-dried spices. I didn't wake up to the lingering odor of freshly made tortillas for breakfast or even sit down with the family to grind *nixtamal* into fresh masa. But that doesn't deter me from developing my palate, trying new techniques, or tasting something that might look or sound a little weird.

In the following section, we've given brief descriptions of items featured in this book that may be obscure in some areas or that most home cooks may not work with on an everyday basis. As globalization continues, you'll probably get familiar with these items as they become more readily available in your local grocery store. After all, remember how obscure cilantro was about twelve years ago?

ACHIOTE PASTE

This paste is made of ground annatto seed, cornmeal, vinegar, salt, spices, and usually a little dye to give it more color. It can be found in the dry-food section of just about any Mexicatessen or Indian market. We use Marin Brand, which comes in a 14-ounce block, but there are other reputable brands out there. Most brands include some sort of natural preservative that allows the paste to hold for quite some time if wrapped in plastic and refrigerated. One block will make about ten batches of Achiote Rice as outlined in our recipe. The red color and earthy flavor of the paste come from the ground annatto seed, which grows inside a small red husk and is used for everything from curing disease to dying clothes.

AGAVE MEAD

Mead is a rich honey wine that comes sweet, medium, or dry. It is usually still but is available sparkling, and can be found in about seventeen different styles from Bochet (burnt or charred) to Capsicumel (spiked with chiles) to various varietals. The one we use is made with blue agave, the type of cactus used to make tequila, and can be ordered from Mountain Meadows Mead (see page 207). Because we use mead for deglazing pan sauces and in sangría, we recommend being adventurous.

AGAVERO

Agavero is a tequila liqueur that can be found in most high-end liquor stores. The liqueur is a blend of blue agave reposado and añejo tequilas that is flavored with the leaves of the damiana plant and aged for a long time in oak. The damiana leaves give the liqueur its bittersweet complexity, and some Oaxacans will claim that they act as an aphrodisiac, arousing a sedate passion in both men and women. These effects may be further enhanced by the 32 percent alcohol of the spirit. A 750 ml bottle should run about $35 and is a great addition to any bar for cooking or simply sipping after dinner.

BANANA LEAVES

These are most commonly sold in flat 1-pound plastic packages (10 by 16 inches) and are found in the freezer section of just about any Latin American or Asian market. They'll hold for a long time when frozen, but you have to be somewhat careful when storing because they can be brittle. One pound of leaves is plenty for any of the recipes in this book.

Banana leaves only take a few hours to defrost but if you're planning ahead, it's best to defrost them in the refrigerator overnight. Sometimes there will be a thick, fibrous rib running along the length of the leaf, which needs to be trimmed out before cutting the leaf into squares for tamales. The leaves are packed in a little salt, which some people wash or wipe away, but we don't mind it for savory recipes. There is a very aromatic quality to the leaves, which permeates meat, fish, and masas when baked, steamed, or grilled.

CACHAÇA

Cachaça is a Brazilian spirit distilled from unrefined sugarcane juice (as opposed to molasses, which is used for rum). The juice is fermented in a wood or copper container for about three weeks, boiled down three times to a concentrate, and then distilled. The drink is 40 percent alcohol and not very pleasant for sipping, but is great for mixing or substituting in any application where rum would be used.

CANELA

Everyone is familiar with cinnamon, but we wanted to note some of the differences between varieties. Most people in the States associate cinnamon with cassia, an aromatic bark also known as Chinese cinnamon. This spice is sold ground or as thick sticks or quills that are rolled from both long ends.

True cinnamon, however, is called canela or Ceylon. It is also sold ground or in quills, but the bark is much thinner, lighter in color, and rolled only from

BANANA LEAVES

CHAYOTES

TOP TO BOTTOM:

QUESO OAXACA, QUESO FRESCO,
AND QUESO COTIJA

one end. The taste and aroma of canela are much softer and more complex than cassia, and add a subtle citrus overtone to both sweet and savory dishes. Canela can be found in most ethnic markets, Mexicatessens, and well-stocked spice stores.

CHAYOTE
. . . .

If the tomato is a vegetable in the culinary world and a fruit in the botanical world, then where in the world does a chayote fall? Also called the christophene or vegetable pear, the chayote comes in a number of different varieties, including yellow and spiny, but the only ones I've ever come across are the pale green chayote with puckered ends. Depending on the store, you'll find them either displayed next to the pears or the zucchini.

Chayote can be baked or sautéed, but we like to dice it fine and use it raw in salads since the skin, almondlike seed, and crisp, juicy texture contrast nicely when mixed with corn and tomatoes.

CHEESES
. . . .

QUESO COTIJA This is an aged cheese that was originally made with goat's milk but today is more commonly made with cow's milk. It is white, semi-firm, and easily found in the refrigerated section of most urban grocery stores and just about all Latin American markets. The cheese is salty and is usually crumbled over black beans, *fideo*, salads, or tacos. It is often compared to Parmesan or feta, both of which may be substituted if necessary. Depending on the density of your cheese, it can be crumbled by hand or run along the small holes of a grater.

QUESO FRESCO This is another cow's milk cheese, with a slightly grainy feel and a nice, fresh acidity and creaminess balanced by a moderate saltiness. The cheese is packed in brine in tubs, similar to fresh mozzarella or farmer's cheese. Most brands of *queso fresco* won't melt, but they should still soften upon heating.

QUESO OAXACA This is a cow's milk cheese with mild acidity, low salt intensity, and somewhat soft texture. It has a low melting point, so it doesn't extrude a lot of grease or separate when melted. *Queso Oaxaca* is usually sold in plastic-wrapped balls (a bit smaller than baseballs) or braids in the refrigerated section of many grocery stores and just about all Latino markets. The cheese shreds well on the large holes of a grater or can simply be torn apart into strands or larger pieces.

Although Cheddar cheese was inappropriately associated with the rising popularity of Mexican cuisine in the United States, melted on everything from canned refried beans to deep-fried burritos, the availability of this authentic product is thankfully reclaiming its culinary importance and place in most Mexican restaurants.

CHICHARRONES
. . . .

Most people in the States associate *chicharrones* (crispy pork rinds) with the snack section at mini-marts and may think that they only come sealed in plastic bags and dusted with red barbecue powder. However, *chicharrones* do play a traditional role in Mexican cuisine and are often sold in the *carnicería* or meat market. *Chicharrones* can occasionally be found fried in large sheets in Latin American markets or *carnicerías,* and can sometimes be found prepared but not fried in stores or online.

The tough pork skin is smoked, dried, and rendered before being deep-fried, resulting in its trademark puffiness and unctuous, rich crispiness. *Chicharrónes* can be stored at room temperature for a few weeks (or longer if held in an airtight container) before the fresh crackly crunch begins to resemble Styrofoam. Their popularity has risen in the U.S. since they were declared a "no-carb" snack for dieters, so their availability and acceptance should continue to increase.

. . . .

There are a plethora of fresh and dried chiles in the culinary world and all serve some integral part of Cajun, Creole, Indian, Asian, and other cuisines. We just happen to be fortunate as Californians to have the majority of the world's crop grown (and consumed) by our neighbors in Mexico. Some chiles are matured and dried on the plant while others are traditionally hung and dried on a *ristra,* or chile string. Thicker-skinned pods, such as the jalapeño, can be dried in a dehydrator or hot-smoked over wood (see chipotle chiles, below).

When dried chiles are purchased, they should be fully intact with dry skins and discernable stems. They should be free of blemishes and be slightly pliable. Chiles are best stored in airtight containers and will usually last for about six months, depending on the humidity of your pantry. When held too long or in excessive humidity, they are favorite targets for tiny moths and weevils.

Be careful when working with chiles as they produce capsaicin—the chemical that produces chiles' well-known burning sensation. Capsaicin also releases endorphins when we eat chiles. It is produced and mostly stored in the veins and seeds of the chile, which can be removed to decrease the heat. (Capsaicin is also extracted to create pepper spray.)

When we first opened Doña Tomás, one of our cooks, Hilda, introduced us to an old wives' tale from Mexico that has worked quite well for us over the years. Should you happen to accidentally rub your eyes while working with chiles or experience a little too much fire in your mouth, place a tablespoon of salt under your tongue and it will suppress the burning.

Mark Miller of Coyote Cafe in Santa Fe probably commented best on the overall properties of dried chiles in his concise *Great Chile Book.* He compares the chile's individual properties—smoky, fruity, and spicy—to the elements of a chord—bass, treble, and high notes. Therefore, each chile has a different character just as each chord has a different sound, which is why we've tried to give a brief description of each of the chiles featured in this book. We've essentially written the music so it's up to you, the artist, to practice and play with the many different chiles in order to make the tune.

. . . .

ANCHO This chile is 4 to 5 inches in length and 3 inches wide at the stem end (*ancho* means wide in Spanish). It is dark red or mahogany with a very wrinkly skin. Anchos are ripened, dried poblano chiles, which is why they have such a nice fruity complexity. They are often used for enhancing salsas and are the chile of choice for stuffing as rellenos. Anchos are often mislabeled as pasilla chiles, which are similar in color and wrinkly texture, but are much larger and thinner.

CHILE DE ÁRBOL This chile is only 3 to 4 inches long and $1/2$ inch in diameter, with a glossy brick red appearance. It's not very big but its heat intensity is enhanced when toasted and added to sauces. The chile is often grated and used as a powder; we like to mix it with other dried chiles when making purées. The aroma of these chiles reminds me of freshly cut grass; when used sparingly, this flavor element can translate to your sauces.

CHIPOTLE The smoked and sauced *chipotles en adobo* have become so popular in the United States that they can be found in almost all grocery stores in 7-ounce cans. Chipotle chiles themselves are simply jalapeño chiles that have been ripened, dried, and smoked; they can be found in most Latin American markets. Most commonly, however, the smoked chiles are packed in an adobo sauce of tomato, vinegar, garlic, and salt. *Chipotles en adobo* are the only kind we call for in our recipes. Any leftovers can be refrigerated in a plastic container for up to a few weeks.

GUAJILLO Along with the ancho chile, this is one of the most popular dried chiles used in our book and in much of Mexican cuisine. It's about 5 inches in length and 1½ inches wide with a very gradual taper; it has a pointed end, flat red color, and smooth skin. The flavor can be rather sweet and somewhat smoky, while the heat intensity is moderate. The skins on many dried chiles, especially this one, can be tough, so we often run any purée through a fine-mesh strainer before adding it to sauces or soups.

MULATO The mulato is a type of dried poblano that is seldom found fresh; it is ripened and dried right on the plant. Its smoky flavor is an integral component of most moles. Much like the ancho chile, the mulato is 4 to 5 inches in length and about 3 inches wide, but the shoulders are not as broad as the ancho and the skin is not quite as wrinkly; its complex flavor is also not as fruity as that of the ancho. If you have difficulty distinguishing between an ancho and a mulato, hold the chiles up to a light—the ancho will have an orange to reddish tint while the mulato will be chocolaty brown.

NUEVO MEXICO These chiles come in a variety of colors and names—green, red, purple (eclipse), yellow (sunrise), orange (sunset), *chile colorado,* and dried California—and miniature versions of each are often used to make *ristras* (chile strings) and wreaths. When our recipes call for *nuevo mexico* chiles, we're referring to the 6-inch-long, 2-inch-wide, cherry-colored chile with the extremely thin, smooth flesh (the chile is translucent when torn open). The aroma is of dried fruits and herbs and the chile is probably most widely used as the flaked topping applied to pizzas. It's also popular in a dried, powdered form.

PASILLA (CHILACA) These chiles may also be labeled as *chile negro* or mislabeled as ancho chiles. The skin is actually shiny and black (as opposed to anchos' mahogany) and the chile is more elongated (5 to 6 inches in length) and much narrower (only 1 to 1½ inches wide) than the ancho. Although the skin is wrinkled like the ancho, the creases aren't as tight or abundant. The pasilla is simply a dried *chile chilaca,* which is rarely found fresh in the United States but is used both fresh and dried throughout Mexico. Pasillas, like anchos, have a complex fruity flavor with moderate heat intensity; their brightness and acidity are almost berrylike.

PASILLA DE OAXACA This may be one of the tougher chiles to come by as it is only grown in Oaxaca. It is shiny red in color and much shorter than a pasilla (only 3 to 4 inches in length) but similar in width and shape. The natural smoky character of this chile is often compared to that of the chipotle, although the heat is much more intense and lingering. This chile is mainly used for a regional relleno, but we actually toast it and blend it into our house salsa. Most store clerks won't know what you're asking for unless they're from Oaxaca or authoritative on Mexican cuisine, so we recommend keeping your eyes peeled during market visits or ordering *chiles de Oaxaca* from online sources or from the Chile Guy (see page 207).

CHILE POBLANO

Poblanos can be found in the produce section of just about any grocery store in the United States these days. Although poblanos and green bell peppers are similar in size, poblanos have darker green, thinner flesh and are more triangular in shape. The chiles can be eaten raw but are often roasted and skinned or dried. When ripened and dried, poblanos are referred to as ancho chiles.

The flesh of poblanos takes to roasting quite nicely and, much as with bell peppers, the flavor becomes more complex and rounded after cooking. The durable nature, smoky complex flavor, and mild heat of this chile make it ideal for stuffing, which is why it is often used for rellenos. Poblanos will hold refrigerated for a week or two when raw but only a few days after being roasted.

CHORIZO

This is another Mexican item that has gained such great popularity in the United States that most people are familiar with it, but not everyone has cooked with it. This sausage can be found in the refrigerator or freezer section of just about every supermarket, but it's one of the few items you'll most certainly want to buy from the Latin American market or *carnicería*. The chorizo found in most grocery stores tends to lack flavor and has a poor texture from too large a grind and not enough fat.

Chorizo's red color usually comes from the inclusion of a ground chile purée (usually guajillo), paprika, and sometimes achiote. A good-quality sausage will remain vibrant red when cooked and will get quite loose and watery if rendered without the skin. We've found that sausages less than 3 inches in length tend to be of higher quality than the larger or *longaniza* ones.

CORN HUSKS

These can be found dried (sometimes fresh) and sold by weight at most Latino markets and even in the ethnic sections of some urban supermarkets. We only use dried corn husks in our recipes, but for more ideas and recipes, *Tamales 101* by Alice Guadalupe Tapp is an excellent resource. A half pound of husks costs about $2 and will make somewhere between 60 and 100 tamales, which is good because once you become proficient you'll definitely want to make more. The husks hold for a long time in plastic wrap but will mold in extremely moist environments.

FOIE GRAS

Fatty duck or goose liver is definitely not an item you will find in your average grocer's freezer. There are only two producers of foie gras in the United States, one in Sonoma, California, and the other in the Hudson Valley of New York. This delicacy can be found fresh or frozen in airtight packaging or tins at high-end specialty grocers and a number of online sites. You'll find different grades of foie gras available; we recommend using grade A or B.

Any leftover odds and ends should be diced, sautéed with a few shallots, and worked into some room temperature butter. This can be used to sauté spinach or greens or to finish sauces with a little extra decadence.

HALIBUT CHEEKS

The cheeks we use in the restaurant come from the large Alaska or Pacific halibut, which can grow up to 8 feet long and weigh as much as 500 pounds. The season runs from March to October; they're often available fresh on the West Coast throughout the summer but may be more difficult to find in other parts of the United States. Most fishmongers and larger supermarkets carry halibut cheeks both fresh and frozen. Frozen cheeks can also be purchased online, but it may be more practical (and economical) to substitute scallops or regular fresh halibut fillet.

HERBS

AVOCADO LEAF These leaves are bright green when fresh and can grow quite large. Found in the spice section of most Latin American markets, they are dried and cut into pieces slightly larger than bay leaves. Avocado leaves are used to flavor masa, grilled meats, stews, and sauces and are aniselike in flavor. The anise flavor can be enhanced by toasting and grinding the leaves immediately prior to use. It is common to find little nubs or balls on the dried leaves, which are left behind by the insects that inhabit the trees and are harmless (just toast and grind them with the leaves). Some chefs say these imperfections enhance the flavor of the leaves, although that may just be an excuse to avoid picking through them.

AVOCADO LEAVES

The leaves of the Hass avocado trees that grow here in the States are supposedly flavorless, so the one in my yard must not be a Hass because we've been toasting and grinding these leaves for quite some time and deriving a good bit of anise flavor from them. *Hoja santa* in the powdered form is a good substitute for avocado leaves, although we started using avocado leaves a few years ago because we couldn't find *hoja santa*.

EPAZOTE This herb can be found fresh or dried in just about every Latin American market. The leaves are long, green, and serrated. We coarsely chop the fresh leaves like cilantro in the few recipes it's called for in this book. The herb is very pungent in its fresh form, smelling somewhat like kerosene, but it loses most of its aroma after the oils have dried out. These oils are said to be carcinogenic in large quantities, but since none of our recipes calls for more than two sprigs (the equivalent of 1 to 2 teaspoons), we can only imagine it being a gastronomically unpleasant death trying to consume enough to poison oneself.

Epazote was once used to cure hookworm and is still sometimes cooked with beans because of its ability to decrease their flatulent qualities (we, however, don't add it to our beans). If you can't find epazote, we recommend substituting escarole or arugula.

HOJA SANTA Also known as the "root beer plant" because of the flavor resemblance to sassafras, these 12-inch velvety leaves grow wild in many areas of the South, where the climate is warm for most of the year. I successfully grew some *hoja santa* plants in my Berkeley garden one summer; they were beautifully climbing and flowering until the gardener ripped them all out. Needless to say, he's no longer my gardener.

A few years ago, we had trouble finding fresh *hoja santa,* but these days many more produce markets in Latin American neighborhoods are carrying it fresh and sometimes even frozen. The fresh and frozen leaves are preferable to the dried or powdered forms since you'll get more of the herb's peppery characteristics from the natural oil in the leaves.

MEXICAN OREGANO There are as many types of Mexican oregano as there are names for the herb (wild sage, Mexican marjoram, and so on), which are all related to each another botanically. The most important distinction between oreganos for our purposes is that between the Mexican and Mediterranean herb. Mediterranean oregano is the one that most Americans would be familiar with; it has tiny, sweet leaves with a tinge of anise flavor and is found fresh in the produce section of most grocery stores, and dried on just about every spice shelf in the country. Most Mexican oreganos have much larger, tougher leaves and are only found dried.

The flavor of Mexican oregano is more pungent than that of its Mediterranean cousin and the aroma is floral. Both of these aspects are enhanced when the herb is rubbed between the palms before being added to soups and sauces. Sautéing Mexican oregano with the onions and vegetables of a sauce will help soften the herb and enhance the flavor. Because it is dried, Mexican oregano can be held for up to six months before the oils start to dissipate. It is easily found in any Latin American neighborhood store that sells spices.

HUITLACOCHE

American farmers refer to this bulbous, grayish-black fungus as corn smut, which may sound a little better than the direct translation of the Aztec word, which happens to be something like "raven's excrement." Neither label comes close to describing the slightly smoky, delicate flavor and delectable texture of this exotic fungus. It can be found canned in most Latin American grocery stores, sometimes fresh depending on where you are in the country. More elaborate Latin American markets will sell it frozen throughout the summer and fall, or you can sometimes buy it online, which can end up costing as much as $30 a pound. We have heard that there is an experimental program in Florida and Pennsylvania to cultivate the fungus. And it does turn out that we often purchase our product from Burns Farms in Groveland, Florida (see page 207).

If you can find *huitlacoche* fresh, buy it on the cob, cut it off, roughly chop it, and freeze it in bags for up to six months. We use it in quite a few recipes so you should make a point of trying it at least once. Substitute a mixture of wild mushrooms if you have difficulty finding *huitlacoche*.

LARD

Fresh, refrigerated lard is sold by the cup at most Latin American grocery stores (where it is usually called *manteca de cerdo*) and butchers'. You can also make your own by purchasing unsalted fatback, pulsing it in a food processor, and rendering it over low heat for a few hours. As a general rule, 1 pound of fatback will make about 2 cups of lard. Fresh lard will hold for a few months in the refrigerator.

Any type of rendered animal fat, such as bacon or duck fat, can be substituted, but will add a smokiness and saltiness that may work well for dishes such as refried beans, but not suit a delicate tamale dough. Although it is often shunned as being unhealthy, fresh lard actually contains less cholesterol than butter does. The hydrogenated version of lard found in virtually every grocery store should be avoided. The stuff is loaded with trans fats and lends a terrible aftertaste to most foods.

MASA

Most Mexicatessens and *tortillerías* will carry a number of different types of masa; our collection of recipes simply calls for two—*masa quebrada simple* for Sweet Tamales (page 53) and *masa fina simple* for Salt Cod Tamales (page 154), tortillas, *sopes*, and *garnachas*. We've provided definitions for the most commonly available masas to help you weed through what's out there.

Masa dough consistency and texture will vary depending on the *tortillería* and sometimes even within the *tortillería* itself due to changing ingredients, climate moisture, and so on. When you're making tortillas on a regular basis, it's ideal to find a *tortillería* that produces a fairly consistent masa.

Fresh masa should be held for no more than two days after it's purchased; the dough quickly begins to sour and alter its character. It should be wrapped in plastic to prevent its drying and picking up other scents in the refrigerator. Masa does not freeze well in its raw form, but holds wonderfully once the tamales have been prepared. Because masa is so cheap, it's a good idea to buy more than is called for in each recipe, just in case there are any mishaps. Any leftovers can be used for *sopes*, tortillas, or even dumplings for soups.

MASA FINA SIMPLE A finely ground masa with almost a playdough-like consistency, *masa fina simple* dough should be moist and firm, not wet or tacky. If the masa is too dry, work a little bit of water into the dough with a paddle and mixer. If it is too wet and sticky, mix in a little masa harina or let it aerate for a half hour before working with it.

MASA HARINA The dried corn flour found in most Latin American markets and mainstream supermarkets is masa harina. It is great to keep a box of it on hand for dusting *masa fina simple* when it gets too tacky to work with. Although some chefs recommend masa harina as backup for fresh masa, tortillas made with it tend to come out dry and gritty and tamales can be heavy and dense.

MASA PREPARADA This masa, used to make tamales, has the lard already whipped into it. It is often shunned by chefs because they feel it's better to add your own fat in order to control quantity and quality. We don't feature this masa in our book because we only use it for savory meat tamales, whereas we use butter or oil as the fat for sweet, vegetarian, and seafood tamales. We do, however, purchase this masa for our restaurants because our *tortillerías* provide us with an excellent product.

MASA QUEBRADA SIMPLE The literal translation of *quebrada* is "broken"; with sauces and masas, it often refers to something with a coarse texture. The word *simple* should be pronounced as sim'-play, not sim'-pul, when ordering at the *tortillería*. This masa tends to be more wet and tacky than *masa fina simple* and is nearly impossible to press into tortillas. This coarse-grind masa still has some of the pedicel (part of the corn plant that supports the kernel), which imparts a little more texture and character to *corunda*-style tamales in which the flavoring ingredients are mixed into the masa. It won't work for other applications, such as tortillas, that need a smoother masa.

MUSHROOMS

There are some seventy-odd species of wild mushrooms found throughout Mexico and foraging for them has become so popular that there are now mushroom tours available to gourmands, vacationers, and mycologists.

If you're not a trained forager, the best places to find wild mushrooms are farmers' markets and specialty grocery stores. Wild mushrooms should be refrigerated, preferably wrapped in paper. If you must keep them in a plastic bag, cut some holes in it for ventilation; the mushrooms will spoil and become slimy if held in something airtight.

CHANTERELLES The season for chanterelles varies between July and February, depending on the climate. There are several species of this mushroom, ranging from pale yellow to bright orange; the most popular is the golden chanterelle. The caps are rather small and trumpet shaped and are anywhere from ½ to 6 inches wide. The gills should run all the way down onto the stem. The flavor of chanterelles is said to be similar to that of apricots, with a very fresh floral aroma and less earthiness than criminis and morels. Any dirt and pine needles should simply be brushed off; washing chanterelles before cooking them dilutes their flavor and makes them soggy.

MORELS Perhaps the most popular wild mushroom, morels are available fresh from April to July and are found dried in abundance year-round. The distinctive look of morels is characterized by the honeycomb texture of the caps. Fresh morels should feel like dry (not hard) sponges and have an earthy smell to them.

When picked properly, morels are cut at the base so there should not be excess dirt. To clean the mushrooms, split them in half, remove any foreign matter or worms with a paring knife, reserving as much of the base and stem as possible, and wipe the cap clean. You shouldn't ever have to run them under water.

PORCINI The porcini season begins in September and can run until June, depending on the weather. Porcinis can be quite large, similar to the size of portabellas, but their flavor is sweeter and much less earthy. You can sometimes find them frozen at specialty stores, and almost always dried. Frozen porcinis are usually preferable to the dried version, although they need a longer cooking time because they produce more liquid. Dried porcinis should be saved for dishes such as risotto that are more dependent on flavor than texture.

Fresh porcinis should have large brown caps with firm white stalks. The underside of the caps should be white; a green or yellow color is the sign of overly mature mushrooms. Porcinis should be wiped clean with a damp towel; avoid running them under water or you'll dilute the flavor. Halve the stem and cap and check for worms and wormholes before slicing; the worms usually start in the stalk and work their way upward. They are harmless so simply discard any you might find.

NIXTAMAL (HOMINY)

Fresh hominy is dried corn that has been treated with lime and partially cooked to have the hull and germ removed. *Nixtamal* is essentially the same thing, but retains the germ and therefore some nutritional benefits. Hominy and *nixtamal* are most commonly used in Mexican cooking for *pozole* and menudo. For our cooking purposes, the two are one and the same as long as they're purchased fresh from a Latin American grocer's refrigerator. Canned, shelf-stable hominy should be avoided; it is simply *nixtamal* that has been soaked in a lye solution and cooked further than the fresh product. The reason it is preferable to cook or "flower" the *nixtamal* directly in the *pozole* or soup is because the fresh kernels give off starches that give the broth additional body, similar to cooking potatoes in a chowder. Fresh *nixtamal* can only be refrigerated for a few days and has the best flavor when used immediately after purchase.

NOPALES

Nopales are the paddles of the prickly pear cactus and can often be found fresh at farmers' markets and at Latin American grocers. *Nopales* are cultivated year-round but are mostly harvested during the spring and summer months. Fresh paddles should be about ¼ inch thick, vibrant green in color, and somewhat rigid—similar to most green vegetables. They can be refrigerated for a few days; after that they become flaccid and lose quite a bit of their flavor intensity. Like most vegetables it's best to store them refrigerated in their raw state. Be sure to cut up the *nopales* right before cooking (sometimes bags of diced are sold in the market) in order to prevent them from extruding their sticky juices and oxidizing. Because of the sharp spines, some cooks wear heavy-duty rubber gloves when prepping large batches. *Nopales* have the best flavor when lightly oiled and grilled. Cooked *nopales* will keep, refrigerated, for no more than a day or two.

PEPITAS

Pepitas is the generic term for the seeds from a variety of different pumpkins in a variety of different forms—hulled, unhulled, toasted, flavored with chile, salted, unsalted, raw, or any combination of the above. In this book, we only call for hulled raw *pepitas,* which can be found in most health food stores and Latin American markets and many supermarkets.

Like most nuts, these seeds have a very high oil content, so they should be stored at room temperature in a sealed container for no more than a few months. Since they burn easily, it is better to toast them on the stove top in a sauté pan than in the oven.

PILONCILLO

Also labeled as *panela* or *panocha, piloncillo* is light or dark unrefined sugar made from sugarcane (the type of cane determines whether the sugar will be light or dark). The sugar is crushed, heated to evaporate the liquid, then dried in cones ranging from three-quarters of an ounce to three-quarters of a pound. You'll usually find 3-ounce cones in Mexicatessens and Latin American markets in a wicker basket next to the herbs and spices. Since the cones are extremely hard, they need to be cut apart with a serrated knife or melted into liquid for use. Light or dark brown sugar may be substituted if necessary, but their heavy molasses notes don't match up to the soft, subtle, caramel sweetness of *piloncillo.*

SALT COD

It's pretty rare to find salt cod in a mainstream grocery store, but some larger fish counters will stock it or can order it for you, as will local fishmongers and European specialty stores. Salt cod can cost as much as $12 a pound, but one box will make two batches of our Salt Cod Tamales recipe (page 154). If possible, select white pieces of

flesh rather than the stringy yellow tail pieces, but you may not have much choice when buying small quantities.

Even after being defrosted, pieces of salt cod will be rather dense and stiff because they've been so well cured in salt. The meat will become much more tender and flaky after it has been soaked, drained, rinsed, and cooked.

Salt cod will hold refrigerated for quite some time but it's best to keep it frozen. If you buy a 1-pound box, soak half of it to use right away and freeze the rest for later use.

TOMATILLOS

Most people are familiar with tomatillos in some form or another, perhaps the most common being a bowl of tangy salsa verde accompanying corn chips at the local Mexican restaurant or cantina. In their raw form, tomatillos range between the size of a cherry tomato to the size of a plum, but you'll usually find them about golf ball size. Fresh tomatillos come wrapped in their dry papery husks. The smaller tomatillos are sweeter, but try not to choose ones that don't fill out their husk as this is a sign of immaturity.

Although the husk is dry and ranges from yellow to brown, it should have a fresh appearance and not look shriveled or decrepit. The skin of the fruit under the husk is sticky and needs to be rinsed in cold water. The fruit itself should be firm. You'll inevitably come across a few blemishes or spots, which can be cut away if small enough; otherwise discard the whole tomatillo.

Tomatillos should be roasted in a small shallow pan with garlic and onion until the skins blacken and split. Much of the juice will squirt out and caramelize, which is why we often deglaze the pan with a little water and add it back into the sauce. The caramelized sugars will take away from the green color of the sauce, but the sweet, complex flavor is far too yummy to wash down the sink.

Tomatillos can also be boiled gently in water, but remove them before the skins split or you'll lose a lot of the flavor into the water. If puréed in their raw form, tomatillos are usually cut with something like avocados to mellow their intense acidity.

TOMATOES

At Doña Tomás and Tacubaya, we use a variety of specialty tomatoes. Summer is often a favorite time of year for California culinarians for the abundance of heirloom tomatoes, if for nothing else. We use Early Girls for just about everything since they are usually the first to hit the market and are available throughout the season. If you aren't raising plants in your backyard, it's highly improbable you'll find anything sweeter or juicier.

Whatever type of tomato you choose to work with, be sure it is ripe and juicy, not hard or green. (Green is okay for Green Zebras, but they still shouldn't be hard.) A hard tomato will still ripen if picked too early, but it won't develop any of its natural sweetness or juiciness off the vine, leaving the overall taste acidic and off balance. The skin should be thin and the meat should be firm but give some resistance, like a water balloon that can't fit another drop. Depending on your location, you'll probably find tastier tomatoes at farmers' markets than at grocery stores.

In the summer, we serve heirloom tomato salads and chilled heirloom tomato soups. Even in winter, we lucky Californians still get some decent vine-ripened and Roma tomatoes from Mexico, where they are a perennial crop. We limit these winter tomatoes to roasting and puréeing, mostly for salsas. Much like when roasting tomatillos, we blacken the skins in a hot oven with onion, garlic, and chiles and deglaze the caramelized sugars in the pan with a little water to get as much flavor as possible.

Store fresh tomatoes uncovered at room temperature; do not refrigerate them unless they've been cut or puréed.

EQUIPMENT

All of the recipes featured in this book are from one of our two restaurants, where we have a large griddle to toast chiles, an industrial tortilla press to make quesadillas, a deep fryer to fry taquitos and mole ingredients, a salamander (overhead broiler) to melt *queso fundido,* convection ovens to evenly bake cakes and breads, and a large grill that's always fired up for carne with wild mushrooms or ears of corn. These recipes may have been born in these kitchens, but they were not conceived here. We use modern equipment to simplify our lives and manage the significant amount of production we face on a daily basis, but we want to make sure you can repeat our successes in your own kitchen.

In the following pages, we've attempted to outline a few pieces of equipment that you really will need. Some of the equipment, such as the tortilla press, serve a specific use and will probably only be useful with this type of cuisine but other pieces, ranging from a ten-dollar lime press to a ninety-nine-dollar five-speed blender, are versatile tools for other cooking applications.

In addition to these items, any well-stocked kitchen should have: wooden spoons, rubber spatulas, metal spatulas, whisks, slotted spoons and skimmers, a good set of stainless steel or copper pots and pans with lids, baking sheets, cake pans, cooling racks, several 9 by 11-inch baking sheets, casserole dishes for baking and serving, cutting boards, a colander, a vegetable peeler, a can opener, and, last but not least, a good set of sharp knives. Not having this basic equipment can make life in the kitchen a challenge, just as having too much of it can clutter the kitchen and make it impossible to find anything.

BLENDER

A blender will be one of the most helpful pieces of equipment for many of the recipes in this cookbook. Chiles for sauces are always puréed in a blender (usually after toasting) rather than a food processor because blending does a better job of breaking up the leathery skins and pulverizing the seeds. A blender will also liquefy tomatoes, tomatillos, avocados, and fruits; it can be useful in emulsifying vinaigrettes and aioli; and is used for a number of other applications in Mexican cooking.

There are easily as many types of blenders as there are uses for them. A 5- or 6-cup blender will allow you to make most of our recipes without having to blend in batches. A minimum of 5 speeds with a 500-watt motor will blend through just about everything. Try to choose one with a stable metal base and a durable, thick glass cup so you can see how the blending is coming along.

CAST-IRON SKILLET

Much like an iron *comal* or griddle, a large cast-iron skillet is an indispensable piece of equipment that will provide you with a lot of use and versatility. A 9-inch skillet is more than sufficient for panfrying and deep-frying, but a 12-incher will provide more surface area when frying salsas and moles. If properly seasoned after each use with a little oil and kosher salt, these pans will last generations. Use a bristle brush and a little hot water to scrub away any stuck food, and be sure to wipe the pan dry with a towel to avoid rusting.

COFFEE GRINDER

For our purposes, a coffee grinder is actually a spice grinder, not essential for the kitchen, but certainly nice to have around for powdering coriander, peppercorns, chiles, and avocado leaves. While some chefs claim that a mortar and pestle gets better flavor out of spices, hand-grinding (especially in large batches) can be rather impractical.

Start with high-quality herbs and spices that haven't been sitting around too long, and grind them right before use to get the best flavor for your dishes. If you're cooking at least two or three recipes a month from this book, a coffee grinder reserved for spices will come in handy.

COMAL OR FLAT IRON GRIDDLE

A *comal* is one of the most important pieces of equipment in traditional Mexican cuisine, used for cooking tortillas directly over a fire. Historically made out of clay or earthenware, modern models are thin, 9-inch cast-iron disks. They come in a variety of styles—sometimes with a small lip or handle and more recently in a 17-inch-long model that can be placed over two burners on the stove top. Along with a blender, a *comal* rates up there as one of the most useful pieces of equipment for success with many of the recipes in this book.

We recommend the oblong 17-inch model or any other long, flat, iron griddle that allows for a good amount of surface area when charring chiles, making the bases for *sopes* or *garnachas*, or cooking more than one tortilla at a time. For most applications, the *comal* works best at medium or medium-high heat. Too much heat for too long will sometimes cause a skillet to warp. Season your *comal* by rubbing it with a little bit of canola oil and kosher salt over a moderate flame after each use. It can be scrubbed with hot water and a brush, but only when absolutely necessary. Try to stay away from soap and cleaners since the material is porous.

ELECTRIC MIXER

We use KitchenAid mixers at both our restaurants and homes and recommend this brand simply because they're built to last. The 4.5-quart bowl with 250 watts is enough to whip cake batter, mix cookie dough, or paddle masa for any of the recipes in this book, but if you really like to do a lot of

baking you may want to consider the 6-quart model. The mixer comes with a dough hook, paddle, and wire whip (the latter two are what we call for in our recipes) and most models have available meat grinder attachments if you want to make your own chorizo or sausage.

FOOD PROCESSOR

Food processors are not as essential for our recipes as are *comales* and blenders, but they can certainly come in handy. We use our food processor to blend sweet potatoes for Camote (page 140), chop nuts for cookies, purée black beans, and even make aioli. Many models even have attachments that can finely shred cabbage, grate cheese, or mince vegetables. Usually an 11- to 12-cup bowl with a 500-plus watt motor will do the trick for home use. As long as the processor comes with a blending and cutting blade (most come with many more attachments) it should be more than sufficient to stand up to the recipes in this book.

RUBBER BAKING MAT

Made of fiberglass and silicone, rubber baking mats are used to line baking sheets so that your food doesn't stick to the pan; they can be purchased just about anywhere that kitchen supplies are sold. They are indispensable for baking sugarcoated pineapple, soft cookie batters, and pumpkin brittle. Be sure to measure your pans before buying your mats since they come in a number of shapes and sizes.

STRAINERS

Every serious cook who enjoys making sauces or stocks should have both a China cap and a chinois strainer. A good China cap is made of perforated stainless steel and is great for straining tomato and chile sauces since it allows some of the pulp to pass through—giving the sauce some body. A good chinois is composed of fine-mesh stainless steel and is perfect for straining thickened emulsified sauces. The chinois also works well for duck or shrimp stocks, since the bones or shells need to be pressed against the sides of the strainer to extrude all of the flavor. A good chinois can be costly, anywhere from $70 to $130, but will provide a lifetime of use if taken care of properly.

TORTILLA PRESS

If you want to try your hand at working with fresh masa, you'll absolutely need a tortilla press. There are two types of presses generally available at Mexicatessens and Latin American markets—a 7-inch metal model with "Hecho en Mexico" embossed across the top plate, and a larger wooden model with an "Hecho en Mexico" sticker somewhere on the handle or base. We prefer the wooden model since the large base gives a little more stability, but if you're cramped for kitchen space, the smaller metal model works fine. Either way, after use, be sure to wipe your press clean of any residual masa since it will mold and stink after a time.

TORTILLA STEAMER

Every evening at Doña Tomás, we set up a steamer on our two back burners and use it to heat and cook our chiles rellenos and tamales. It doesn't take much to set up a very effective steamer at home—all you'll need are two equal-sized baking sheets or pans, a wire cooling rack or perforated pan that sits comfortably inside the baking sheets, and a few kitchen towels (avoid towels with heavy dyes as they may bleed into the food).

Place one of the baking sheets over two burners on your stovetop and fill it with hot water to a quarter inch below the rim. Place the wire cooling rack into the baking sheet and line it with a kitchen towel. The rack keeps the food suspended above the water and the towel keeps everything moist. Bring the

water to a boil, then decrease the heat to achieve a simmer; it should also be producing steam. Place the tamales or rellenos on the towel in an even layer, then cover the whole contraption with the other baking sheet to trap the steam.

Rellenos will take between 8 and 10 minutes to cook, while most tamales will take 15 to 20 minutes, depending on the level of steam. It's extremely important to have two pans of the same size in order to trap the steam or the items sitting directly over the burners will cook faster than those around them. Also be sure to leave a little space between items to allow the steam to circulate— cooking in batches is always recommended over stacking and layering. During cooking, be careful to monitor the water level so that it all doesn't evaporate away. For sweet tamales, it also helps to cover them with a towel during cooking to infuse the masa with a little more moisture.

There are two cautionary measures to be aware of when working with this type of steamer. The first and most important is to be careful when removing the lid to the steamer. Since the steam is being held in a confined area it has the tendency to billow out when released and can cause severe burns. Be sure not to have your face, arms, or hands over the steamer in anticipation of getting a glimpse of your rellenos or tamales.

The second caution to take is regarding disassembly. To avoid moving a baking sheet full of hot water, allow it to cool for a while before disassembling the steamer.

DRINK EQUIPMENT

Just as any kitchen needs to be stocked with more than forks, knives, and plates, so does a bar need to be stocked with more than spirits, limes, and glasses to make most of our drinks. You don't need to become a full-service bar, but a few standard items will make your drink-mixing life much easier.

As mentioned earlier, you'll need a blender for puréeing fruit for aguas frescas. Some type of drip coffee pot or press is needed to make our breakfast coffee drinks, and you'll obviously want a sharp paring knife and cutting board for the fruit, limes, and garnishes. It is a good idea to keep a small container of coarse salt and another of coarse sugar on hand for margaritas, lowriders, and Tomás Collinses.

We have recorded most of our recipes in "counts" since we feel that mixology is based more on taste than on exact quantity. The acidity level and juiciness of limes vary throughout the season, alcohol percentages change from brand to brand, and effervescence differs from one tonic to the next. We recommend purchasing a few pour spouts (fancier spouts will even dispense a designated quantity of liquor) and using them for your more frequently used liquors. For our drink recipes, 5 counts with a pour spout equals about 1½ ounces, a dash is the equivalent of 5 milliliters, and 3 lime halves generally equal 1 ounce of lime juice.

. . . .

COCKTAIL SHAKER A shaker and strainer are used for just about all of the cocktails featured in this book. A good shaker is made of a thin layer of stainless steel, allowing it to fit snugly over a pint glass to create a tight seal during shaking. Most cocktail strainers have built-in strainers on top, but we never use them. It is much more practical to strain drinks directly from the pint glass with a wire-coil stainless steel strainer that conforms perfectly to the glass. These strainers may or may not be sold with the cocktail shaker, but both can be found at most kitchen-supply stores and liquor outlets.

LIME PRESS Made of cast iron, good-quality lime presses can be found online or in most Latin American markets and Mexicatessens. A lime press is definitely not a necessity, but it will make juicing limes much easier and more efficient in regard to both time and juice yield.

MOLINILLO If you want to make authentic Mexican hot chocolate, you'll need the special wooden whisk called the *molinillo*. These beautifully adorned implements look more like decorative clubs than pieces of kitchen equipment. The handle is affixed to a wider area that is notched and surrounded by one or several loose wooden rings. When the handle of the *molinillo* is rolled rapidly between the palms of the hands, the notches and rings agitate the hot chocolate, causing it to froth up. *Molinillos* can be found in most Latin American markets and some specialty kitchen shops and can vary greatly in price depending on the design, engraving, type of wood, and perceived value by the purveyor. They can often be purchased online and are found sold in kits with Mexican chocolate and *piloncillo*.

MUDDLER A muddler is simply a wooden dowel that looks something like a baseball bat and is used to crush ice and ingredients such as fruits and herbs. We most commonly use our muddler to crush mint leaves with ice and simple syrup for mojitos—the crushing of the mint helps to release the natural oils that give the drink its intense flavor. The nubbed end, which would be the end you would hold if it were a baseball bat, is the end that is supposed to go in the glass and do the crushing work. Muddlers can range from 5 to 10 inches in length and can be found at most specialty kitchen stores and liquor outlets. They can also be found at some fishing supply stores since they're used to club live fish after being caught, although we don't recommend using the same muddler for both fishing and drinking.

TECHNIQUES

Most of the techniques we use in our kitchens are based on culinary practices that have been at the heart of Mexican cuisine for centuries—the toasting of chiles; the roasting of vegetables; the whipping, kneading, and frying of masa.

You'll notice there are certain practices we do not provide recipes or techniques for—such as preparing masa, pulling fresh cheeses, and stuffing sausages. Although we may toy around with these techniques from time to time in our restaurants (we've even ground our own cocoa nibs to make chocolate) it is simply out of curiosity and respect for the ingredients. We love Mexican cuisine, but making a consistently good masa on a daily basis is a craft within itself and not our focus or intent. What we do want to do here is introduce you to the techniques you'll need to become comfortable with in order to successfully prepare the recipes in this book.

CHILES, TOASTING AND PEELING
....

Knowing how to toast and peel chiles is essential to success in Mexican cooking. For many chiles, such as the fresh poblano, toasting is done to enhance flavor and remove the tough leathery skin. For dried chiles, such as the ancho, mulato, and *pasilla de Oaxaca*, toasting makes the flesh a little more pliable and enhances the chiles' smoky flavor characteristics. And, finally, some smaller dried chiles, such as the *chile de árbol*, are toasted not only for flavor but to crisp up the skin and flesh in order to make chile flakes or powder.

There are probably about as many ways of toasting chiles as there are chile varieties, but we're only going to extrapolate on two, one for dried and one for fresh.

DRIED CHILES Each dried chile has its own cooking time, but we generally call for 2 to 3 minutes. Actual cooking times can depend on how high the heat is, what type of pan is being used, how long the chile has been dried, the chile's initial water content, the age of the chile, and the current humidity, so really what it comes down to is toasting a few and getting a feel for your desired aroma, appearance, and pliability.

At the restaurants, since we cook in such big batches, we toast dried chiles on large, flat griddles, although we don't grease them like we do for fresh. At home, it's more practical to toast your chiles on the stove top. Heat a small, dry sauté pan over high heat for about 1 minute. Place the chiles in the pan and decrease the heat to medium-high. With a pair of tongs or a spatula, press the chiles into the pan to dry-sear the entire surface. Be careful because the capsaicin in the chiles is being toasted here and can be irritating when inhaled; it is always beneficial to have the fan on high and keep your nose away from the pan.

Continue to press the chiles into the pan, flipping them every 20 to 30 seconds as the flesh begins to darken slightly and the aroma becomes tobacco-esque. Many of the chiles will puff up as they begin to heat. Once the chiles are relatively brown, carefully remove them from the pan with tongs. When they are cool enough to handle, break the stem off with your fingers and shake the seeds out of the pod. The only time we do not remove the seeds is when we're making chile powders or sauces with smaller chiles, such as the *chile de árbol*, or when we are making rellenos with ancho chiles.

Once the seeds and stems are removed, place the chiles in a bowl and cover with hot tap water. To make sure the chiles are fully submerged, you can place a small plate in the bowl to hold them under water. Some chefs recommend using the soaking water for sauces, but we find it bitter more often than not and don't suggest this practice. Once the chiles have been rehydrated, they are ready to be puréed, chopped, or stuffed.

FRESH CHILES The ideal way to toast fresh chiles to get the best flavor and the most even blistering would be over a wood fire, but this isn't always practical for home cooks. Toasting fresh chiles over a gas burner can impart the flavor of the heat source, which isn't exactly desirable, and deep-frying can infuse the flesh with too much fat, leaving the pepper greasy. After eliminating these options, we recommend simple panfrying as the best way to toast fresh chiles.

At our restaurants, we will sometimes toast 20 to 30 fresh chiles at a time, so we use a large grill. Your best bet at home is a *comal,* small griddle, or cast-iron skillet. Heat your pan over high heat and grease the surface with a light coating of nonstick spray or brush it with a little oil. Decrease the heat to medium and place the chiles on the hot surface. They should crack or pop a few times, and the ridges of the chiles that make contact will begin to blacken.

Slowly toast the chiles, turning them every few minutes as the skins continue to blacken. Some of the indented surfaces won't make contact at first, but as the flesh begins to soften, more and more of the chile will collapse and allow the skins to evenly blacken all around. It may be necessary to prop the chiles against each another to get some of the edges and corners.

In order to evenly blacken and blister as much of the skin as possible, it is important to spray the griddle from time to time since oil helps conduct heat. The entire cooking process should take anywhere from 20 to 30 minutes. A brief word of caution: it is possible to overcook your chiles! Although you want the skins to blacken thoroughly and evenly, if the chiles are cooked too long or at too high heat, the flesh will begin to break down and the chile will fall apart during the peeling process.

After the skins have been blackened, place the chiles in a paper or plastic bag for about 20 minutes. This will trap the heat, creating steam that will pull the skins away from the flesh. Remove the chiles from the bag and gently peel off the skin, trying to keep the chile intact if using for rellenos. To remove the seeds, cut a slit in the side of the chile with a paring knife and gently cut out the seedpod near the stem end. It is pretty easy to get the whole seedpod out with one cut. Although rinsing the chiles under water can help remove any difficult skin and loose seeds, we recommend against this practice since it also will flush out some of the flavor. Plus a few patches of skin and seeds never hurt anyone.

DEEP-FRYING

Every day at the restaurants, we put our fryer to work frying large batches of corn tortillas for chips. We do use the fryer for other preparations, such as taquitos, carnitas, apple fritters, and churros, but contrary to popular belief, not all Mexican cuisine is dumped into a basket and submerged in hot oil.

Unfortunately, deep-frying is often overdone in Mexican restaurants—where you'll find everything from fried peppers filled with cheese to meat-and-rice filled burritos (chimichangas). And most home cooks shun deep-frying since the same items are available through the magic of frozen products and a microwave oven.

Many people avoid frying food at home because of the associated health issues; others simply are afraid of contending with 350°F oil temperatures. Compared to steaming or poaching, frying may be unhealthy, but when enjoyed in moderation like everything else, foods prepared this way are simply delicious. When properly planned, the procedure is also simple to execute and the results are much more rewarding than a bag of potato chips or an order of French fries.

The best pan to use for frying at home is a cast-iron skillet because it transfers heat well and is easy to clean, but any stainless steel or copper pan with 2- to 3-inch straight sides will suffice. We used a 9-inch skillet when testing the recipes in this book and found that 3 to 4 cups of canola oil will be enough to submerge most of the fried items in 1 to 2 batches (some recipes, such as churros, cook better in 5 to 6 batches). The keys to successful frying are having enough oil to submerge the items at least halfway, maintaining the oil at 350° to 375°F, and not crowding the pan with too many items at once. An overcrowded pan will cause the oil temperature to drop, which will yield soggy, greasy food.

To avoid spattering and overflow, never fill your frying pan more than halfway with oil. Heat the oil over high heat for 7 to 8 minutes, then check the temperature by placing a dollop of batter or a piece of the item to be fried into the oil. If the oil is hot enough, the batter or food should produce a consistent and immediate flow of bubbles without too much crackling or popping. Once the oil has reached this ideal temperature, adjust the heat to medium-high to maintain the appropriate heat.

Always have a skimmer, slotted spoon, or pair of tongs ready to transfer fried items to a paper towel–lined plate for draining. If the food is to be salted, do it right when it is fresh out of the pan since the heat will help melt the salt evenly. If fried items have to be held for a short time when entertaining, place them in a 200°F oven, but you really should try to consume fried foods, especially batter-fried foods like rellenos and shrimp tacos, right away in order to fully appreciate the crisp texture.

Any leftover oil that isn't too cloudy or dark can be cooled and saved in a glass jar for your next batch of frying, but shouldn't be used for other forms of cooking or reserved for more than a few weeks.

TORTILLA PRESSING

We would love to be able to jot down a definitive set of rules to make your first experience with making fresh tortillas with masa a successful one, but unfortunately, those rules do not exist. Where you buy your masa, your method of pressing (by hand or machine), and the *comal* or griddle used to cook the tortillas will all affect your final product. But when it comes down to it, the one element that will differentiate machine-pressed tortillas from traditional hand-pressed ones is practice.

We get plenty of practice at both restaurants, pressing pounds of masa dough every day for tortillas, *sopes*, and *garnachas*. At Doña Tomás, we use a crank machine with adjustable rollers that produces beautifully even tortillas of any thickness. At Tacubaya, we use a wooden press, which is what we recommend for home use. It is much more practical for smaller batches, much easier to store and take care of, and works just as well as the crank machine with a little finessing and practice.

The first step to successful tortilla making is to divide the masa into equal parts. At Tacubaya, we use a #30 ice cream scoop to make balls about 1¼ inches in diameter. When pressed, this size ball will yield a 5-inch diameter tortilla. One of the most common mistakes when making tortillas is scaling the masa too large, which makes it difficult to handle, usually resulting in a torn tortilla. One and a half pounds of *masa fina simple* will make 15 to 20 (5-inch) tortillas.

Before pressing the dough, it is important to line the plates of the press with plastic so that the dough

TOASTING FRESH POBLANOS

TORTILLA PRESSING

doesn't stick to the press. Thin grocery store bags and resealable bags work well for this. The key element in lining the press is cutting the bag to the appropriate size. If the sheets of plastic are too large, they will crease and fold on the tortilla. For 5-inch tortillas, you will need two 6-inch plastic circles.

The next concern before pressing is making sure that the dough itself is not too wet. If it is, it will stick to the plastic lining during the pressing process and become impossible to work with. We recommend working a little masa harina into the dough if it seems too tacky. Beginners may also want to dust the plastic sheets with a little masa harina to help prevent sticking. After enough practice, you'll feel comfortable leaving the masa harina on the shelf.

Center one of the plastic circles on the bottom plate of the press and place a ball of masa in the middle. Slightly press the masa ball down with your hand and cover with the other piece of plastic. Close the cover and apply enough pressure to the handle to flatten the dough to a 5-inch tortilla; you'll get a better idea as to how much pressure is needed after the first one or two tortillas. Lift the top of the press and gently peel the top plastic off. Flip the tortilla onto the palm of your hand and gently pull away the second sheet of plastic.

Flip the unwrapped tortilla directly onto a heated, lightly greased griddle or *comal*. Cook for 1 to 2 minutes, until the masa congeals and forms. Flip the tortilla and cook the other side for 1 to 2 minutes, then stack in a cloth-lined bread basket. Until you gain more practice, give yourself 30 to 40 minutes to get a 2-pound batch of masa rolled, pressed, and cooked—the process does move along much faster once you get used to it. Because of limited stove and kitchen space, you might want to cook your tortillas about an hour before serving, then hold them in a towel-lined basket and reheat them on the griddle just before sitting down to eat.

DESAYUNO

BREAKFAST

If you happen to be wandering through your local market and run across fresh cactus paddles, we highly recommend (carefully) grabbing a few for this wonderful breakfast dish. *Nopales*, or cactus paddles, are somewhat comparable to okra, although the flavor is more acidic and less bitter and the texture is crisper. See page 25 for more information about buying and handling *nopales*. Serve with puréed black beans and fresh corn tortillas.

HUEVOS REVUELTOS NORTEÑOS

• SCRAMBLED EGGS WITH TOMATO AND NOPALES •
• SERVES 4 •

1 large (4- by 10-inch) nopal
1 tablespoon canola oil
Kosher salt
2 small heirloom, vine-ripened, or
     Roma tomatoes, diced
1 serrano chile, chopped
2 tablespoons unsalted butter
8 eggs, beaten
¼ bunch cilantro, stemmed and chopped

. . . .

Gently hold the base of the *nopal* with your thumb and forefinger or with a pair of tongs and hold it parallel to a cutting board. Place a sharp knife at the base, just at the skin line, and cut in a sawing motion away from you to remove the thorns, taking off as little of the skin as possible. Turn the paddle over and repeat on the other side.

Lay the paddle flat on the cutting board and carefully cut away any remaining thorns around the rim of the paddle. Immediately discard the thorns to avoid any sticky accidents. Cut the cactus into ½-inch squares.

Place a nonstick sauté pan over high heat and add the oil. When the oil has just reached its smoking point, add the diced *nopales*. The high heat will help retain crispness and facilitate even cooking. Stir with a wooden spoon, then cover and cook for 2 minutes.

Remove the lid, sprinkle with some salt and decrease the heat to medium-high if necessary. After 4 to 5 minutes the *nopales* will begin to turn a vibrant yellow-green and extrude their juices. Replace the lid and continue to cook for 4 to 5 minutes, until all of the liquid has been reabsorbed.

Add the tomatoes and chile and sauté for about 1 minute. Add the butter and stir until melted, then add the eggs and a little more salt. Stir constantly with a wooden spoon until the eggs begin to coagulate. Cook the eggs for 3 to 5 minutes to desired doneness and adjust the seasoning. Transfer to a serving plate, sprinkle with the cilantro, and serve at once.

This dish has been a hit on our Tacubaya menu ever since we opened and, more important, is one of the few things the Schnetz kids will eat. The flavors are bold and the concept traditional; a dish that any egg-, sausage-, and toast-eating American can appreciate. For those in search of a little more culinary adventure, see Diana Kennedy's *From My Mexican Kitchen* for a recipe for making your own chorizo sausage. Serve the eggs with a side of puréed black beans and fresh corn tortillas.

HUEVOS REVUELTOS CON CHORIZO

• SCRAMBLED EGGS WITH MEXICAN SAUSAGE •
• SERVES 4 •

1 tablespoon unsalted butter
2 (3-inch) chorizo sausage links,
　　meat removed from casing
10 eggs, beaten
Kosher salt
Freshly ground black pepper
¼ bunch cilantro, stemmed and chopped

. . . .

Place a large skillet over high heat and add the butter. When the butter is melted, add the chorizo and decrease the heat to medium-high. Stirring constantly and breaking up any clumps with a wooden spoon, cook for about 3 minutes, or until the meat is browned and the fat has been rendered out of the meat.

Pour off some of the fat if there seems to be too much (it can always be incorporated back into the eggs at the end of the cooking process). Increase the heat to high and whisk in the eggs, stirring constantly with a wooden spoon to prevent sticking and browning. The seasoning from the sausage will taint the eggs to a terra-cotta or brick color.

Cook the eggs for 3 to 5 minutes, until they begin to coagulate. Carefully adjust the seasoning with salt and pepper; most chorizo is both salty and spicy so you might not need much. Stir in the cilantro when the eggs are the desired doneness, and transfer to a serving platter. Serve at once.

This is a playful adaptation of the traditional Mexican breakfast of *huevos rancheros; divorciado* refers to the two distinct salsas adorning the fried eggs. The salsas should definitely be made a day or two ahead to simplify morning assembly. Any leftover salsa would go great with poultry or fish entrées or simply with fresh tortilla chips. Serve the huevos with hot refried beans and fresh corn tortillas.

HUEVOS DIVORCIADOS

• FRIED EGGS WITH TOMATILLO AND TOMATO SALSAS •
• SERVES 4 •

SALSA ROJA

4 heirloom or vine-ripened tomatoes
1/2 cup sliced white onion
3 cloves garlic
3 ancho chiles
2 chiles de árbol
2 tablespoons canola oil
Kosher salt

TOMATILLO SALSA

1 cup tomatillos (about 6 ounces)
1/2 cup sliced white onion
3 cloves garlic
2 fresh serrano chiles, stemmed
1/4 bunch cilantro, stemmed
1 pinch ground allspice
Kosher salt

1/4 cup unsalted butter
8 eggs
Kosher salt
Freshly ground black pepper

To prepare the salsa roja, preheat the oven to 350°F. Place the tomatoes on a baking sheet and sprinkle with the onion and garlic. Bake for 45 minutes, until all the vegetables are nice and brown with a fully roasted aroma.

Place a small, dry skillet over medium heat. Add the anchos and *chiles de árbol* and toast for 2 to 3 minutes, pressing them into the pan and turning occasionally with tongs to prevent burning, until they are tobacco brown. While the chiles are still hot, remove the stems and seeds from the anchos and just the stems from the *chiles de árbol*. Submerge in a bowl of hot water for 15 minutes to rehydrate.

Drain the soaked chiles and place them in a blender with about half their volume of fresh water. Blend on high for 1 to 2 minutes, until a fine purée is achieved; it should be thick enough to coat the back of a spoon. Return the skillet to the stove top over high heat and add the oil. Add the chile purée, decrease the heat to medium, and cook for 5 to 10 minutes to bring out the flavor of the purée.

CONTINUED

Place the roasted tomatoes, onion, and garlic in the blender and pulse on medium speed until slightly chunky but well puréed. Add to the chile purée on the stove and bring to a boil to incorporate the flavors. Season with salt and remove from heat. Allow to cool completely. The salsa can be refrigerated in an airtight container for up to 3 days.

To make the tomatillo salsa, soak the tomatillos in cold water for a few minutes and then peel off the husks. Place the tomatillos on a baking sheet and sprinkle with the onion, garlic, and serrano chiles. Place in the oven at the same time as the tomatoes for the salsa roja are cooking, and bake in the 350°F oven for about 50 minutes, until the vegetables are nice and brown with a fully roasted aroma.

Transfer the tomatillos, onion, garlic, and chiles to the blender and add the cilantro and allspice. Pulse in the blender to desired consistency, then season with salt and allow to cool completely. The salsa can be refrigerated in an airtight container for up to 3 days.

To assemble the *huevos divorciados,* place each salsa in a small saucepan and warm over medium heat. Place a large skillet over high heat and add the butter. Break the eggs into the skillet and fry for 4 to 7 minutes, or to desired yolk firmness, and season with salt and pepper. Transfer the eggs to individual plates or a serving platter. Cover half of each serving of eggs with a spoonful of tomatillo salsa and half with a spoonful of salsa roja. Serve at once, accompanied by the hot beans and tortillas.

Mexican Hot Sauce

EXTRA HOT

Tamazula

FL. OZ. (140 mL

IMPORTED FROM MEXICO

CHOLULA

HOT SAUCE

One of the great things about opening our taquería in Berkeley was being able to put this breakfast dish on the menu. The contrasting textures of the crisp tortilla chips and soft eggs, along with the mild, smoky heat of the guajillo sauce, give this recipe a character unlike any other breakfast.

The guajillo sauce has a very pronounced chile flavor and it works just as well with enchiladas and carne asada. It's best to make the sauce a day or two in advance so that the eggs are the only ones scrambling first thing in the morning.

CHILAQUILES

• SAUTÉED TORTILLA CHIPS IN GUAJILLO SAUCE WITH EGGS AND CHEESE •
• SERVES 4 •

GUAJILLO SAUCE

1½ ounces dried guajillo chiles

⅓ cup canola oil

6 cloves garlic

3 cups chicken broth (page 201)

¼ teaspoon ground cumin

½ teaspoon dried oregano

¼ teaspoon freshly ground black pepper

Kosher salt

CHILAQUILES

2 tablespoons canola oil

10 ounces corn tortilla chips

1½ cups grated Monterey Jack, mozzarella,
  or Muenster cheese, or a mixture

2 tablespoons unsalted butter

8 eggs, beaten

Kosher salt

¼ cup thinly sliced white onion

⅓ cup crumbled Cotija cheese

¼ cup chopped cilantro

¼ cup crema (page 198) or sour cream,
  for serving

. . . .

To prepare the sauce, place a dry sauté pan or skillet over medium-low heat. Add the chiles and toast for 2 to 3 minutes, pressing them into the pan and turning occasionally with tongs to prevent burning, until they are tobacco brown. While the chiles are still hot, remove the stems and seeds and submerge in a bowl of hot water for 20 to 30 minutes to rehydrate.

Return the sauté pan to low heat and add the oil and garlic. Slowly sauté the garlic for about 5 minutes, swirling occasionally, until lightly browned. The oil should bubble very gently around the cloves during cooking. Remove the cloves from the pan and reserve the oil for later sautéing use.

Place the stock in a large pot and bring to a boil over high heat. Drain the chiles and place in a large blender. Add the garlic, cumin, oregano, pepper, a few pinches of salt, and about 1½ cups of the chicken stock. Blend on high for about 30 seconds, until a thick paste begins to form. Gradually add the remaining 1½ cups of stock until the sauce achieves the consistency of a thin tomato sauce—thick enough to coat the chips but thin enough to be somewhat absorbed. Adjust the seasoning to taste.

To prepare the chilaquiles, place a skillet over high heat and add the oil. Add about 2 cups of the guajillo sauce and bring to a boil, then add the tortilla chips. Sauté the chips in the sauce for about 3 minutes, stirring gently with a wooden spoon as the chips absorb the sauce. Continue to add sauce until all the chips are well coated but not soupy; you may not use all the sauce. Add the grated cheese and stir once or twice until lightly melted. Transfer to a serving platter or 4 individual plates.

Place a separate nonstick pan over medium heat and add the butter. When the butter is melted, add the eggs, season with salt, and cook for 3 to 5 minutes, to desired doneness. A softer egg tends to contrast the bite of the chips a little better. Evenly spread the eggs over the top of the chips, sprinkle with the onion, Cotija cheese, and cilantro, and drizzle with crema. Serve immediately.

This is a simple relleno that makes a great breakfast with tomato sauce and tortillas. While these instructions call for frying the rellenos, they can be steamed just as easily. We do recommend frying them since the heartiness of the potatoes goes well with a crisper batter.

CHILES RELLENOS CON PAPAS

• ROASTED POBLANO CHILES STUFFED WITH POTATOES •
• SERVES 4 TO 8 •

1½ pounds Yukon gold potatoes, unpeeled

¼ cup heavy whipping cream, warmed

½ cup grated Cotija cheese

½ cup grated Monterey Jack cheese

Kosher salt

8 large poblano chiles, toasted, seeded,
    and peeled (see page 34)

BATTER

1⅓ cups all-purpose flour, plus ½ cup
    for dredging

1½ cups mineral water

2 egg yolks

Pinch of kosher salt

2 egg whites, beaten to soft peaks

3 cups canola oil, for frying

SAUCE AND GARNISH

1½ cups tomato sauce, heated (page 203)

¼ cup crema (page 198) or sour cream,
    for serving

12 fresh corn tortillas, heated, for serving
    (page 35)

. . . .

Wash the potatoes and place in a large stainless steel pot. Add water to cover and a few teaspoons of salt. Cover the pot, place over high heat, and bring to a boil. Uncover, decrease the heat to medium, and simmer for 30 to 40 minutes, until fork-tender.

Drain the potatoes in a colander and transfer to a large bowl. Roughly break them into marble-size pieces with a hand masher or large fork. Add the warm cream and stir well. The consistency should be coarse and lumpy. When the potatoes have cooled to room temperature, stir in the Cotija and Jack cheeses and add salt to taste.

Stuff about ½ cup of the potato mixture into each of the roasted chiles, being careful not to overextend the pockets with any too-large pieces of potato.

To prepare the batter, in a bowl, combine the flour, mineral water, egg yolks, and salt and mix well to form a wet batter. Gently fold the beaten egg whites into the batter (together, the whites and the mineral water will aerate the batter).

Place a large skillet over high heat and add the oil. Heat to 350°F or until a drop of batter sizzles when added. Decrease the heat to medium-high to maintain the temperature.

Spread the ½ cup flour out on a plate. One at time, dredge the stuffed rellenos in the flour, being sure to coat all sides, then pat off any excess flour. Submerge the rellenos in the batter so that the chile is completely coated. Carefully place 3 to 4 rellenos in the skillet at a time to prevent overcrowding. Cook for 4 to 5 minutes, turning with tongs 3 or 4 times, until evenly fried and golden brown. The batter should be firm and crisp. Remove from the oil with tongs and place on paper towels to drain.

The chiles can be held in a 200°F oven during the frying process, but keep in mind that the crispiness will soften the longer the rellenos are held. To serve, line a platter or plates with the tomato sauce and top with the warm rellenos. Drizzle with the crema and serve with the tortillas.

This vegetable relleno is best served during midsummer when the corn is fully sweetened and the zucchinis are not too firm or bitter. This is one of the few dishes in which we use red onions as opposed to white—staying true to the components of the inspiration for this recipe, a pasta from Chez Panisse in Berkeley. The tomatillo-guajillo sauce nicely rounds out the dish with its mellow acidic note and enhances the taste of summer. Whether frying or steaming a stuffed chile (this one works well either fried or steamed), it's important to use relatively high heat to prevent the chile from becoming too soft and mushy. The rellenos can be stuffed and refrigerated a day before cooking; however, the batter should be held no longer than half an hour or it will collapse. If you're steaming the rellenos, you can skip the batter preparation.

CHILES RELLENOS VEGETALES

• ROASTED POBLANO CHILES STUFFED WITH ZUCCHINI AND CORN •
• SERVES 4 TO 6 •

SAUCE

3/4 pound tomatillos

1 1/2 small dried guajillo chiles, seeded
and stemmed

1 large clove garlic, peeled

2 white onions, sliced

Kosher salt

6 tablespoons canola oil

1/2 cup diced red onion

Kosher salt

2 cups fresh corn kernels

2 cups diced zucchini

1 tablespoon minced serrano chile

2 tablespoons grated lime zest

1/4 cup chopped cilantro

3/4 pound grated queso Oaxaca

3/4 pound grated Monterey Jack cheese

8 large fresh poblano chiles, toasted,
seeded, and peeled (see pages 35–37)

BATTER

1 1/3 cups all-purpose flour, plus 1/2 cup
for dredging

1 1/2 cups mineral water

2 egg yolks

Pinch of kosher salt

2 egg whites, whipped to soft peaks

3 to 4 cups canola oil, for frying

1/4 cup crema (page 198) or sour cream,
for serving

12 fresh corn tortillas, heated, for serving
(see page 35)

. . . .

To prepare the sauce, soak the tomatillos in cold water for a few minutes and then peel off the husks. Drain and place in a saucepan over high heat. Add the chiles, garlic, and onions and cover with enough cold water to fill the pan. Bring to a boil, then decrease the heat to medium and simmer for 5 to 10 minutes, until the tomatillos begin to lose their vibrant color and the garlic and onions become partially translucent. You do not want the tomatillos to split and lose their juices in the water, so watch carefully and remove from the heat just before the skins begin to break.

Drain the vegetables and transfer to a blender with a few pinches of salt. Blend quickly on high speed until smooth. Set aside until ready to use or allow to cool and refrigerate in an airtight container for up to 3 days.

Place a large sauté pan over high heat and add 2 tablespoons of the oil. When the oil is hot, add the onion and sauté for 1 minute. Decrease the heat to medium-high, season with salt, and continue to sauté for about 4 minutes, or until translucent. Transfer to a large bowl. Add 2 tablespoons of the oil to the same pan and add the corn. Season with salt and sauté for 4 to 5 minutes, until the corn is tender. Transfer to the bowl with the onions. Add the remaining 2 tablespoons oil to the same pan and add the zucchini. Season with salt and sauté for 2 to 3 minutes, until the skin becomes vibrant green and the flesh is slightly tender. Transfer to the bowl with the onions and corn and mix well. Stir in the serrano chile, lime zest, and cilantro.

Allow the vegetable mixture to cool slightly, then add the *queso Oaxaca* and the Jack cheese and stir well. Season to taste with salt, keeping in mind that some of the salt intensity will be set off by the unseasoned roasted chiles and the fat of the cheese.

Stuff about 1/2 cup of the vegetable mixture into each of the roasted chiles, being careful not to overfill and tear the pockets or leave the chiles too empty, which will cause them to collapse.

CONTINUED

If you are steaming the rellenos, skip the next three paragraphs. If you are frying them, prepare the batter.

To make the batter, in a bowl, combine the flour, mineral water, egg yolks, and salt and mix well to form a wet batter. Gently fold the whipped egg whites into the batter (together, the whites and the mineral water will aerate the batter).

To fry the rellenos, place a large skillet over medium-high heat and add the oil. Heat to 350°F or until a drop of batter sizzles when added. Decrease the heat to medium-high to maintain the temperature.

Spread the ½ cup flour out on a plate. One at a time, dredge the rellenos in the flour, being sure to coat all sides, then pat off any excess flour. Submerge the rellenos into the batter so that the chile is completely coated. Carefully place 3 to 4 rellenos in the skillet at a time to prevent overcrowding. Cook for 5 to 10 minutes, turning with tongs 3 or 4 times, until evenly fried and golden brown. The batter should be firm and crisp. Remove from the oil with tongs and place on paper towels to drain.

The chiles can be held in a 200°F oven during the frying process, but keep in mind that the crispiness will soften the longer the rellenos are held. To serve, line a platter or plates with the warmed tomatillo-guajillo sauce and top with the rellenos. Drizzle with the crema and serve with the tortillas.

If you are steaming the rellenos, prepare a relleno steamer as described on page 30. Stuff the filling into the roasted chiles, being careful not to overfill (tearing the pocket) or underfill (leaving the chile too empty and collapsible). Gently place the rellenos in the prepared steamer with the slits facing up. Cover the steamer and cook over medium heat for about 20 minutes, until the chiles are hot all the way through. Be certain to check and maintain the water level during cooking.

The most definitive ingredient in menudo, tripe, is the stomach lining of a cow, usually from the second stomach (cows have four stomachs for different stages of digestion). Tripe is sold at most *carnicerías* and reputable butcher shops, and has a honeycomb texture ideal for holding copious amounts of broth with each spoonful. It needs to be soaked and rinsed several times before use, and we also let it sit for at least an hour in lime juice and salt water to help break down the rubbery fibers.

Our soup has even made a Cinco de Mayo appearance in the *Oakland Tribune*'s food section, although it was misstated as being a treat my mother would lovingly make for the family, when in reality the thought of tripe makes her shudder.

MENUDO

• SPICY TRIPE AND HOMINY SOUP •
• SERVES 6 •

1 pound tripe, cut into 1/2-inch squares,
    rinsed and drained several times
3 tablespoons kosher salt
Juice of 1 lime
4 dried guajillo chiles
1 cup warm water
4 cloves garlic, chopped
2 teaspoons ground cumin
2 teaspoons canola oil
1/2 white onion, diced
1 teaspoon dried oregano
1 pig's foot
1/4 pound beef marrow bones
6 cups cold water
1/2 pound prepared hominy

GARNISH
1/2 white onion, diced
1/4 head green cabbage, julienned
3 radishes, thinly sliced
1 tablespoon dried oregano
1 lime, cut into thin wedges

. . . .

In a bowl, toss the tripe with the salt and lime juice and cover with cold water. Refrigerate for at least 1 hour.

Place a dry skillet over medium heat. Add the chiles and toast for 2 to 3 minutes, pressing them into the pan and turning occasionally with tongs to prevent burning, until the skins begin to brown and the chiles become soft and flexible and give off their spicy aroma. While the chiles are still hot, remove

CONTINUED

the stems and seeds and submerge them in a bowl of hot water for 15 to 30 minutes to rehydrate. Drain the chiles and transfer to a blender with the warm water, half of the garlic, and the cumin. Process to a smooth purée.

Place a large pot over high heat and add the oil. Add the onion and sauté for 4 to 5 minutes, until translucent. Decrease the heat to medium-high and add the remaining garlic. Rub the oregano between your hands into the pot (grinding the leaves like this releases the flavor). Add the tripe and the chile purée and decrease the heat to low. Cook for 30 minutes, stirring occasionally to prevent scorching and spattering.

Add the pig's foot, marrow bones, cold water, and hominy and increase the heat to high. Bring to a slow boil then decrease the heat to low and simmer gently, uncovered, for 2 hours, until the tripe and hominy are tender. Adjust the seasoning with salt as necessary.

Set aside to cool if not serving immediately; the soup will hold covered and refrigerated for 3 to 4 days. When reheating be sure to stir occasionally over a low flame as the hominy has a tendency to adhere to the bottom and scorch.

To serve, divide the onion, cabbage, and radishes between 6 bowls and crumble the oregano between your palms over the garnishes. Ladle the hot soup into the bowls to wilt the cabbage and radishes, then spike each rim with a lime wedge. Serve at once.

LEFT TO RIGHT: MICHELADA (PAGE 118); MENUDO (PAGES 53-54); CHUPACABRA (PAGE 66).

This sweet tamale is not served for dessert, but is often enjoyed at breakfast with a cup of *café de olla*. We flavor our *tamal dulce* with fresh corn (the white tends to be sweeter and less starchy) and pineapple juice, but you can use more traditional ingredients such as raisins, canela, vanilla, and almonds. Because the ingredients are mixed into the masa instead of being used as a filling (known as *corunda* style) the masa is a little runny, but can be easy to work with if refrigerated for an hour before shaping. For more detailed information on masas, see pages 23–24.

After they're cooked, these tamales can be refrigerated for 2 to 3 days or frozen in their husks for up to 3 months. Frozen tamales shouldn't be defrosted prior to heating; just place them directly into the steamer for 15 to 20 minutes until they are cooked through and soft.

TAMALES DULCES

• SWEET TAMALES WITH FRESH CORN •
• SERVES 6 TO 8 •

1 tablespoon unsalted butter

2 cups fresh corn kernels

Kosher salt

3 pounds masa quebrada simple

1 cup granulated sugar

6 tablespoons pineapple juice

1½ cups plus 6 tablespoons unsalted butter, melted

1 teaspoon ground canela

12 to 24 corn husks, soaked overnight and dried

. . . .

Place a large sauté pan over medium-high heat and add the 1 tablespoon butter. When the butter is melted, add the corn and sauté for 1 to 2 minutes, just long enough to cook some of the starchiness out. Season lightly with salt to taste.

Place the prepared masa in the bowl of a stand mixer fitted with the paddle attachment. Turn the mixer on low speed and work the dough for about 5 minutes. At the beginning, the masa should have the consistency of firm cookie dough. Begin adding the corn, sugar, pineapple juice, melted butter, and canela in small increments as the dough is mixing, alternating ingredients to maintain the dough's stiffness. The pineapple juice and butter will make the dough wet enough to slide off the paddle while the corn and sugar will give it some structure.

Once everything is added, mix the dough at a medium speed for 5 more minutes so that it is fully incorporated and aerated. From time to time, turn the mixer off and scrape down the sides and bottom of the bowl with a spatula. The finished masa should be slightly darker than it started out and be a little stiffer than cake batter but softer than cookie dough. Cover and refrigerate the dough for about 1 hour.

Prepare a tamale steamer as described on page 30. Using an ice cream scoop, place a ¾-cup size scoop of masa in the center of the smooth side of a corn husk. If the husk is too small, overlap 2 pieces in order to create a larger surface area. Flatten the masa with the back of the scoop so that it covers the husk to within 1 inch of the wide end and 2 inches of the tapered end, keeping in mind that the dough will expand as it cooks. Fold

in the sides of the husk; the masa will work as glue to hold them in. Then fold the tapered end up to the open end of the tamale. The dough should be firm enough that, if carefully handled, it will not extrude from the open end of the husk.

Gently place the tamales in the prepared steamer, arranging them so that the tail of the husk is down to prevent unraveling. Cover the steamer and cook over low heat for 20 to 30 minutes, until the dough is cakey and stiff. Do not cook too long or the tamales will be dry and dense. Be certain to check and maintain the water level during cooking.

Carefully remove the tamales from the steamer with tongs and arrange on a serving platter. Enjoy while hot.

ENSALADA DE MELON

• MELON SALAD WITH CREMA AND FRESH MINT •
• SERVES 6 TO 8 •

This salad can be served anytime of day, but you should only make it during the summer when the melons are sweet and ripe. There are a number of melon varieties on the market, and this recipe may serve as the perfect excuse to finally try out a casaba, crenshaw, or ambrosia. This salad has a nice blend of sweet, hot, and savory and can accompany any number of dishes. The melons can be peeled ahead of time, but don't drizzle with the oil and seasoning until ready to serve.

1 cantaloupe, peeled, seeded, and cubed
1/2 honeydew, peeled, seeded, and cubed
2 tablespoons extra-virgin olive oil
1 tablespoon kosher salt
2 teaspoons chile powder
1/2 cup crema (page 202)
1 bunch mint, stemmed and chopped

....

Place the melon cubes on a large platter. Drizzle with the olive oil. In a small bowl, mix together the salt and chile powder and sprinkle evenly over the melon. Drizzle with the crema and sprinkle with the mint right before serving.

Flour is not indigenous to Mexico, but churros are a popular treat in Mexican cuisine. Unfortunately, most Americans have only tasted this breakfast treat in a ballpark or at a hot dog stand, where they inevitably resemble dried-out pieces of cardboard. A true churro should be as rich and full as its culture. When the nomadic shepherds of Spain had no ovens in which to bake bread, they came up with this alternative frying method. When sheep were brought to Mexico, so were the shepherds, who carried with them what many consider to be the perfect accompaniment for *café de olla* or Mexican hot chocolate.

This preparation is not difficult by any means, but it does involve a little bit of precision and attention. You'll need to work quickly when adding the eggs in order to prevent them from scrambling; however, if they're added too slowly they won't properly incorporate. We do guarantee that after tasting a fresh churro, you'll never order one from a hot dog cart again.

CHURROS

• MEXICAN DOUGHNUTS •
• MAKES 20 TO 30 PIECES •

2 cups water
6 tablespoons unsalted butter
1 teaspoon plus $1/2$ cup granulated sugar
$3/4$ teaspoon salt
2 $2/3$ cups all-purpose flour, sifted
2 jumbo eggs
2 tablespoons ground canela
2 to 3 cups canola oil, for frying

. . . .

CONTINUED

In a saucepan, bring the water, butter, 1 teaspoon sugar, and salt to a boil over high heat. Once the mixture begins boiling, reduce the heat to medium and quickly add the flour in thirds, stirring to incorporate after each addition. Keep stirring for 1 to 2 minutes, until the flour is well incorporated, making sure to scrape the bottom and sides of the pan to remove any flour that may stick.

While the dough is still hot, transfer it to a stand mixer fitted with the paddle attachment. Turn the mixer on low speed and mix for about 15 seconds to cool the outside of the dough before adding the eggs. One at a time, add the eggs and mix on low speed, allowing the first egg to incorporate into the mixture before adding the next. The dough will become more elastic, smooth, and shiny after each egg is added. Once the dough is fully mixed, set it aside for about 10 minutes until it is just cool enough to handle. (You don't want it to cool too much or it will be too stiff to pipe.)

On a plate, mix together the canela and the ½ cup sugar for coating. Pour the oil into a skillet to a depth of ½ inch and place over high heat. Bring the oil to 350°F without allowing it to smoke, adjusting the heat as necessary; this should take no longer than 10 minutes.

Spoon one-quarter of the dough into a pastry bag fitted with a large star tip. If the dough is too hot to work with, wrap the bag with a towel to protect your hands. If it gets too cold and stiff, microwave it in a piece of plastic wrap (don't place the metal tip in the microwave!) for about 10 seconds to soften it up. Press the dough to the base of the bag and pipe it out into 8-inch strips directly into the hot oil.

Work in small batches of 5 or 6 strips, cooking each batch for 3 to 5 minutes, gently turning and submerging the churros with a slotted spoon or tongs, until slightly browned and crispy. If the oil temperature is too low, the churros will split before browning. Using tongs or a slotted spoon, remove the churros from the oil and transfer to paper towels to drain for 1 to 2 minutes. While the churros are still hot, roll them in the sugar and canela mixture so that they are well coated. Repeat the entire process with the remaining dough, continuing to pipe and fry in small batches. Do not go to the ballpark and do not pass go, but serve hot.

CLOCKWISE FROM LEFT: CAFÉ DE OLLA (PAGE 65); CHURROS (PAGES 59-60); MANZANAS FRITAS (PAGES 62-63).

This is actually an old Schnetz family recipe that is a great brunch alternative to fruit-filled blintzes or waffles covered with compote. These fritters are the only way I'll ever eat apples since I've never cared for them otherwise—in fact my grandmother once gave me a new suit when I reluctantly but obediently ate a piece of her apple pie. *Cajeta* is a creamy caramel, usually made from goat's milk, that is very popular throughout Mexico. Unlike traditional caramels, *cajeta* tends to be a bit thinner and more refined with a spicy complexity from the canela. It marries well with just about any dessert—especially fried apples. The *cajeta* can be prepared in advance and will hold covered in the fridge for a week or two, while the apples should be prepared the day of serving. Although they vary slightly in flavor, goat's and cow's milk are similar in composition, so it is okay to substitute cow's milk if necessary. Larger Latin American markets will often carry some type of goat's milk, although it may be easier to get it from a neighbor if you live in a rural area.

MANZANAS FRITAS CON CAJETA

• APPLE FRITTERS WITH GOAT'S MILK CARAMEL •
• SERVES 4 TO 6 •

CAJETA
Makes 2 cups

3 cups goat's milk or whole cow's milk
3/4 cup granulated sugar
1/4 cup corn syrup
2 inch canela stick
A rounded 1/8 teaspoon baking soda
2 teaspoons cold water

BATTER

1 egg
3/4 cup milk
1/4 teaspoon salt
1 cup all-purpose flour
3 tablespoons confectioners' sugar
1 teaspoon baking powder
1/3 teaspoon ground canela

5 Granny Smith apples, peeled and cored
1/4 cup granulated sugar
2 tablespoons ground canela
3 to 4 cups canola oil, for frying
Confectioners' sugar, for sprinkling

....

To prepare the *cajeta,* place the milk, sugar, corn syrup, and canela stick in a saucepan and bring to a boil over high heat, whisking occasionally to prevent boiling over. In a small bowl, dissolve the baking soda in the water (this mixture will help bind the caramel). Rapidly whisk the baking soda mixture into the saucepan, removing it from the heat if it threatens to spill over. Decrease the heat to medium and simmer for 45 minutes to 1 hour, until the mixture has cooked down and turned dark brown and thick. Remove from the heat and pass through a fine-mesh strainer, and keep warm.

To prepare the batter, combine the egg, milk, and salt in a bowl and mix well. In a separate bowl, sift together the flour, confectioners' sugar, baking powder, and canela. Slowly add the dry ingredients to the wet ingredients, mixing until there are just a few lumps left. Be careful not to overmix or the batter will become tough and chewy. Set aside for 30 minutes to allow the batter to relax.

Preheat the oven to 350°F. Line a baking sheet with a rubber baking mat. Slice the apples into ¾-inch rings (you should get 5 to 6 per apple) and arrange in one layer on the prepared baking sheet. In a small bowl, mix together the sugar and canela. Sprinkle the top of each apple with a generous layer of the sugar mixture. Place in the oven and bake for 10 to 15 minutes, until the sugar melts and caramelizes. Remove from the oven and allow to cool.

Pour the oil into a skillet to a depth of ½ inch and place over high heat. Bring the oil to 350°F without allowing it to smoke, adjusting the heat as necessary; this should take no longer than 10 minutes. One by one, completely dredge the apple rings in the batter and gently submerge them in the hot oil. Working in batches to avoid overcrowding, cook for 3 to 4 minutes, until browned. Transfer with a slotted spoon to paper towels to drain.

Transfer the apples to a serving platter while still hot, drizzle with the *cajeta,* and sprinkle with confectioners' sugar. Serve immediately.

The unique qualities of this Mexican chocolate drink are due to both the technique and the type of chocolate used. Traditional Mexican chocolate doesn't have added cocoa butter to increase its viscosity, as premium European chocolates do. This extra cocoa butter can leave a residual film on top of the drink. Good Mexican chocolate should be made simply of sugar, cocoa beans, cinnamon, and almonds, with no lecithin or artificial emulsifiers. When melted, the chocolate will have a gritty texture because of its lower cocoa butter content, but it can be melted directly in a pot without having to be coddled over a double boiler.

In order to give this drink its authentic frothy texture, you'll need a *molinillo* (see page 32), is a small turned whisk that looks like an adorned wooden club. Prior to the Spanish introduction of the *molinillo*, the drink was poured from head to toe between two vessels to make it frothy, which requires great accuracy and can be both messy and disastrous if not executed properly. We recommend sticking with the *molinillo*.

CHOCOLATE

• MEXICAN HOT CHOCOLATE •
• SERVES 1 •

2 ounces Mexican chocolate
1 cup whole milk

. . . .

Place the chocolate in a small saucepan over low heat and stir until melted. Add the milk, increase the heat to high, and stir until warmed through. Remove the pan from the heat and completely submerge the head of your *molinillo* in the milk. Rapidly roll the handle of the *molinillo* between the palms of your hands for 1 to 2 minutes, until the milk is frothy. Pour into your favorite mug and enjoy while hot.

This Mexican coffee drink is flavored with a sweet syrup of *piloncillo* and canela. It's traditionally made in an earthenware pot called an *olla,* which enhances its earthy flavor (sometimes a little too much depending on the age of the pot). Much of its customary character still comes through with the following conventional recipe and method.

Café Mexicano is similar to Irish coffee, although the Kahlúa hints at a more Latin flavor, the taste of a different Old Country. Kahlúa adds chocolate and coconut aromas, enhances the coffee flavor, and gives the drink a subtle sweetness. A great hot beverage to enjoy with a weekend breakfast or after dinner.

CAFÉ DE OLLA

• SPICED MEXICAN COFFEE •

• SERVES 8 •

CAFÉ MEXICANO

• SPIKED MEXICAN COFFEE •

• SERVES 1 •

4 (3-ounce) cones dark piloncillo
1 (6-inch) canela stick
1$\frac{1}{3}$ cups water
8 cups brewed coffee

2 ounces Kahlúa
1 cup brewed coffee
2 ounces (4 tablespoons) whipped cream
1 (6-inch) canela stick

Cut the cones of *piloncillo* into 3 or 4 pieces each and place them in a saucepan. Break the canela stick with your fingers into the saucepan. Add the water and place over high heat until the liquid comes to a boil. Decrease the heat to medium and simmer, stirring occasionally, for 45 minutes to 1 hour, until the sugar is melted and a flavorful light brown syrup forms. Pass the liquid through a fine-mesh strainer or chinois and set aside to cool.

Divide the coffee evenly among 8 mugs. Add $\frac{1}{8}$ of the syrup to each cup of coffee and enjoy while hot.

Pour the Kahlúa into a large mug and add the coffee. Top with the whipped cream and garnish with a piece of canela stick for stirring. Enjoy while hot.

The Chupacabra has been feared for centuries by goat farmers and shepherds throughout Mexico and parts of Central and South America. The beast stands somewhere between 3 and 4 feet tall, has razor sharp claws, emits a foul odor from its buttocks, and has a number of deadly incisors or fangs used to pierce animals' necks, sucking the blood out with its long, snakelike tongue.

Although the creature remains elusive and is yet to be photographed or studied, many swear that it exists and is roaming around the countryside. Some even believe it descends from outer space in its very own UFO. It apparently doesn't travel too far north, perhaps because of a poor relationship with Sasquatch.

We don't use any goat's blood in our drink but we're certain if El Chupacabra made his way to Berkeley or Oakland, this is what he'd be having.

CHUPACABRA

• BLOODY MARY •
• SERVES 1 •

4 counts vodka, preferably Absolut
1 dash Worcestershire sauce
Juice of ½ lemon
Juice ½ lime
Juice of ¼ orange
¼ teaspoon hot chile sauce,
    preferably El Yucateco Red
3 ounces (6 tablespoons) tomato juice

GARNISH
1 lemon slice
1 jalapeño chile, slit at the base
1 green onion

Combine the vodka, Worcestershire sauce, lemon juice, lime juice, orange juice, chile sauce, and tomato juice in a pint glass, cover with a cocktail shaker, and shake vigorously. Pour into a fresh pint glass filled with ice and spike the rim of the glass with the lemon slice, jalapeño, and green onion. Drink at once.

ALMUERZO

LUNCH

This delicious soup has been on the Doña Tomás menu since the day we opened. Every time we've tried to replace it with a different tortilla soup, we've been met with hearty resistance from our regular customers. Its pronounced lime flavor is tamed by the savory chicken broth and nicely balanced by the heat of the chiles.

When we make the soup at the restaurant we make huge gallon batches and use our broth for a number of other items on the menu. One 4-pound chicken makes 1½ quarts of broth, but you'll only need a quarter of the meat (about ½ pound, or 2 cups shredded) for this soup. The rest of the meat can be set aside for use in tacos, *sopes*, or enchiladas.

SOPA DE LIMA

• CHICKEN, LIME, AND CHILE SOUP •
• SERVES 6; MAKES ABOUT 1½ QUARTS •

1½ quarts chicken broth (page 201)
1 tablespoon vegetable oil
½ white onion, cut into ⅓-inch dice
1 teaspoon chopped garlic
½ jalapeño chile, chopped
2 heirloom or vine-ripened tomatoes,
    cut into ⅓-inch dice
Juice of 2 limes
1 bunch cilantro, stemmed and chopped
2 cups shredded cooked chicken (see page 201)
About 6 teaspoons kosher salt
2 to 3 cups loosely crushed tortilla chips

. . . .

Place the broth in a large saucepan over medium heat and bring to a simmer.

In a separate soup pot, heat the oil over high heat for 2 to 3 minutes. Add the onion and sauté for 4 to 5 minutes, until translucent, stirring with a wooden spoon to prevent burning. Add the garlic and sauté for 30 seconds, stirring constantly until the aroma is

released. Add the jalapeño and tomatoes, and lightly sauté for 5 minutes. Stir in the lime juice and half of the cilantro, then remove the pan from the heat.

Pour the broth into the pot of sautéed vegetables. Place the pot back on the stove top over high heat until it boils. Add a few pinches of salt, reduce heat to medium, and simmer gently for about 30 minutes, until the flavors completely fuse. Add half of the shredded chicken (reserve the remainder for another use) and simmer for about 5 minutes, adjusting the seasoning with salt if necessary.

Ladle the soup into large bowls and top each with ½ cup of the crushed tortilla chips. Divide the remaining cilantro among the bowls. The garnish must be crispy and fresh and sized so that it fits on a soup spoon and provides appropriate contrast.

The soup can be refrigerated in a covered container for up to 3 days and reheated as necessary, but the tortilla and cilantro garnish should always be added at the last minute.

Long before opening Doña Tomás, the best *sopa de tortilla* I ever had was in little shack off Highway 121 in Sonoma County. But right before opening the restaurant, Dona and I traveled to Oaxaca for ideas and research, and stumbled across three older ladies who cooked in the small kitchen of a restaurant called El Topil. Hands down, they made the best tortilla soup I've ever tasted.

Two years later, I returned with my wife for the Day of the Dead celebrations and took it upon myself to have at least three bowls of El Topil's tortilla soup a day for the entire week. After plenty of testing, the following recipe is as close as my taste buds could come to re-creating the dish, which for me brings back some very fond memories.

SOPA DE TORTILLA

• TORTILLA SOUP •
• SERVES 6; MAKES ABOUT 1 1/2 QUARTS •

2 guajillo chiles

1 ancho chile

1 cup warm water

3 heirloom or vine-ripened tomatoes,
    or 6 Roma tomatoes

2 cloves garlic

1 1/2 quarts chicken broth (page 201)

2 tablespoons canola oil

1/2 white onion, cut into 1/3-inch dice

2 cups shredded cooked chicken
    (see page 201)

Kosher salt

GARNISH

1/4 pound baby spinach

1/3 pound queso Oaxaca, shredded

2 avocados, diced

2 cups loosely crushed tortilla chips

Place a dry skillet over medium heat. Add the guajillo and ancho chiles and toast for 2 to 3 minutes, pressing them into the pan and turning occasionally with tongs to prevent burning, until the skins begin to brown and the chiles become soft and flexible and give off their spicy aroma. While the chiles are still hot, remove the stems and seeds and submerge in a bowl of hot water for about 30 minutes to rehydrate. Drain the chiles and transfer to a blender. Add the warm water and purée until smooth. Leave this purée in the blender.

CONTINUED

Preheat the oven to 350°F. Place the tomatoes and garlic in a small baking dish and roast for about 45 minutes, until the tomato skins begin to blacken and split. The juice will bleed from the tomatoes and caramelize on the bottom of the pan. Add the tomatoes and garlic to the blender with the chiles and purée on high speed for 1 to 2 minutes.

Place the broth in a large saucepan over medium heat and bring to a simmer. Place the baking dish on the stove top over high heat. Add a few ladles of the simmering chicken broth and scrape the bottom of the pan with a wooden spoon to loosen the caramelized tomato bits. Simmer for 1 to 2 minutes, then pour this mixture back into the chicken broth.

Place a separate soup pot over high heat and add the oil. When the oil is hot, add the onion and sauté for 4 to 5 minutes, until translucent. Add the tomato and chile purée, decrease the heat to medium, and bring to a simmer for about 5 minutes, stirring with a wooden spoon to prevent scorching. The consistency should be that of thick marinara sauce. Pass the broth directly through a fine-mesh strainer into the soup pot and gently simmer for 20 minutes so the flavors come together. Add the shredded chicken and simmer for about 5 minutes. Adjust the seasoning with salt if necessary.

To serve, divide the spinach, cheese, and avocado between 6 bowls and ladle the hot soup over each. Top with the tortilla chips and serve immediately.

The soup can be refrigerated in a covered container for up to 3 days and reheated as necessary, but the spinach, cheese, avocado, and tortilla chip garnishes should always be added at the last minute.

This cold soup is refreshing throughout the summer as long as the tomatoes are ripe and the weather is warm. We prefer to use heirlooms because they're sweeter and more flavorful than Romas or vine-ripened tomatoes. Other tomatoes can be substituted but they won't be as tasty unless they're coming from your own garden.

GAZPACHO

• CHILLED HEIRLOOM TOMATO AND CUCUMBER SOUP WITH AVOCADO •
• SERVES 4 TO 6; MAKES ABOUT 1¹⁄₂ QUARTS •

1 large English cucumber, peeled, seeded,
    and coarsely chopped
¹⁄₄ cup red wine vinegar
2 tablespoons extra-virgin olive oil
About 1¹⁄₂ tablespoons kosher salt
4 pounds heirloom tomatoes
¹⁄₂ white onion, diced
3 cloves garlic
1 small jalapeño chile, stemmed and
    coarsely chopped
2 avocados, cut into ³⁄₄-inch dice, for garnish
¹⁄₂ bunch cilantro, stemmed and chopped,
    for garnish

. . . .

Place the cucumber in a blender and purée on a low speed until a coarse consistency is achieved. Add the vinegar, olive oil, and salt and pulse 2 to 3 times to incorporate. Pour into a serving bowl and set aside.

Place a saucepan filled about halfway with water over high heat and bring to a boil. Fill a large bowl with ice water. Stem the tomatoes and slash an X into the skin at the bottoms. Submerge the tomatoes in the boiling water for 30 seconds to loosen the skins, drain, and immediately plunge into the ice bath. Drain again, then peel off the skins. Place a fine-mesh strainer over a bowl. Cut the tomatoes in half crosswise and squeeze the tomatoes into the strainer, using your fingers to extract as many of the seeds as possible. The goal is to remove and discard the seeds while still reserving the precious juice in the bowl.

Working in batches if necessary, transfer the tomatoes and their juice and the onion, garlic, and jalapeño to a blender. Purée on high speed until liquefied and smooth. Pour into the bowl with the cucumber purée, stir well, and adjust the seasoning with salt if necessary (cold soups will often need more salt than hot soups).

Cover and place the soup in the refrigerator for 1 to 2 hours, until well chilled. Ladle into chilled bowls and garnish with the avocado and cilantro. This soup can be refrigerated in a plastic container for up to 2 to 3 days, but is best enjoyed within 24 hours of preparation.

Whenever I travel to Los Angeles, I dine at what I consider to be the finest Mexican restaurant between the Bay and the border. La Serenta de Garibaldi has been one of L.A.'s premier Mexican dining establishments for more than a decade now; the chef/owner Jose Rodriguez specializes in some of the best Mexican seafood in the city. When I first started eating there, I'd look around at everyone enjoying attractive glass goblets of tomato broth filled with scallops, shrimp, and whitefish, but could never seem to find it on the menu. It was like you had to be a part of a special club (or proficient in Spanish) to get a taste of the chef's specials, *coctel de pescados*. Despite my linguistic deficiency and lack of local credentials, I somehow managed to coerce the waiter into bringing me a bowl during each of my visits. And although the dish now headlines the menu, I still feel special every time I dip into a serving.

After making several attempts at emulating the dish, I finally managed to pinpoint the secret ingredient that provides just the right balance between the sweet and sour of the broth, the spice of the fresh chile, and the delicacy of the fish—a common but elusive Mexican ingredient known in these parts as ketchup.

Seafood cocktail is quite popular in the coastal areas of Mexico, especially during Easter when Christians assiduously refrain from eating any form of meat. We like to serve it as an appetizer at Doña Tomás or a light lunch at Tacubaya with fresh local oysters; you can substitute 1 pound of shrimp or other seafood for the oysters. Either way, this broth recipe will complement just about any type of seafood.

COCTEL DE OSTIONES

• OYSTER COCKTAIL •
• SERVES 6 •

1 scant quart vegetable broth, chilled (page 202)
½ cup seeded and diced cucumber
⅓ cup chopped green onion
1 cup chopped vine-ripened or Early Girl tomatoes
1 teaspoon chopped serrano chile
½ cup ketchup
3 tablespoons freshly squeezed lime juice
About 1½ tablespoons kosher salt
18 medium fresh oysters, shucked with
    juices reserved
⅛ cup chopped cilantro, for garnish

. . . .

Place the vegetable broth in a bowl and add the cucumber, green onion, tomatoes, chile, ketchup, and lime juice. Taste and adjust the seasoning with salt as necessary. Cover and refrigerate until well chilled. This broth can be held in the refrigerator for about 3 days.

Place the oysters and their juices in a small sauté pan and cook over high heat for 2 to 3 minutes, until slightly firm but not rubbery. (The oysters could also be baked at 350°F for 3 to 5 minutes.) Place 3 oysters and some of their liquid in each glass bowl and cover with a ladle of the cocktail broth. Garnish with the cilantro and serve at once.

Since Mexico's independence in 1821, the country's flag has been made up of three colors—green, white, and red. Although the crested eagle and format have changed through the years, the colors have remained the same: the green representing the fertility of the land, the white the unity and purity of the people, and the red the blood of its heroes and the price of freedom. These colors are often purposely displayed in traditional dishes using a wide range of colorful ingredients—hominy, tomatillos, red and green chiles, avocados, and tomatoes.

This soup and the next are no exceptions to this patriotic culinary rule. We have, however, only included the red crab *pozole* and the green duck *pozole*. The white, which is often a pork and chicken *pozole*, carries plenty of culinary merit, but in our opinion, is not as flavorfully diverse as its two comrades.

POZOLE DE JAIBA

• CRAB AND HOMINY SOUP •
• SERVES 6; MAKES ABOUT 1 1/2 QUARTS •

1/2 pound prepared hominy (nixtamal)
1 ancho chile
3 guajillo chiles
About 1 quart shrimp broth (page 199)
3 cloves garlic
1/3 teaspoon ground cumin
1/3 teaspoon ground cloves
1 tablespoon canola oil
2 cups finely diced white onion
About 1 tablespoon kosher salt
1 teaspoon dried oregano
1 pound crabmeat

GARNISH
1/2 white onion, cut into 1/4-inch dice
2 tablespoons dried oregano
3 radishes, thinly sliced
1/4 head green cabbage, julienned
1 lime, thinly sliced

Rinse the prepared hominy in a strainer, place in a saucepan, and cover with cold water. Place over high heat, bring to a boil, and then decrease the heat to achieve a simmer. Cook for about 2 hours, until the hominy flowers open.

Place a dry skillet over medium heat. Add the ancho and guajillo chiles and toast for 2 to 3 minutes, pressing them into the pan and turning occasionally with tongs to prevent burning, until the skins begin to brown and the chiles become soft and flexible and give off their spicy aroma. While the chiles are still hot, remove the stems and seeds and submerge in a bowl of hot water for about 30 minutes to rehydrate. Drain the chiles and transfer to a blender. Add 1 cup of the broth, the garlic, cumin, and cloves and purée until smooth.

Place a large soup pot over high heat and add the oil. When the oil is hot, add the onion and salt and sauté for 4 to 5 minutes, until the onion becomes translucent. Rub the oregano between your hands into the pot, grinding the leaves to release the flavor. Add the chile purée, decrease the heat to medium, and fry about 5 minutes, stirring with a wooden spoon to prevent scorching.

Add the remaining broth and increase the heat to high in order to bring to a boil. Decrease the heat to medium and simmer for about 20 minutes. Drain the hominy and add it to the broth, and cook for 20 to 30 minutes to bring the flavors together. This broth can be covered and refrigerated for 3 days without the crab. When reheating, be sure to stir well since the hominy will stick to the bottom of the pan and burn.

To serve the soup, divide the crabmeat among 6 soup bowls. Ladle the hot soup over each. Place the bowls on plates and surround with individual piles of the onion, oregano, radishes, cabbage, and lime.

Duck is not the most common ingredient in Mexican restaurants, then again, you don't often find it in American restaurants either. There are, however, both farm-raised and wild ducks available at some of the *carnicerías* and downtown markets of Mexico. In the United States, you can buy whole birds at most specialty butcher shops, especially around the holidays.

This recipe appeared on our very first Doña Tomás menu back in 1999, so we felt it was important to include it in this collection. Although the soup can be somewhat time-consuming, it's a very fun dish to make and a great way to introduce yourself to Latino ingredients such as epazote and *hoja santa*. Serve this *pozole* with a side of rice.

POZOLE DE PATO
• DUCK AND HOMINY SOUP WITH TOMATILLOS •
• SERVES 6; MAKES ABOUT 1½ QUARTS •

1 (3- to 5-pound) duck
3 tablespoons kosher salt
2 tablespoons dried oregano

TOMATILLO SALSA
2 cups tomatillos (about ¾ pound), peeled
¼ cup water
¼ bunch cilantro, stemmed
1 clove garlic
½ jalapeño chile
About ½ teaspoon kosher salt
½ bunch parsley, stemmed and chopped
1 bunch epazote, chopped
2 tablespoons powdered hoja santa or
    ground dried avocado leaf
2 quarts cold water
1 pound prepared hominy
Kosher salt

GARNISH
½ white onion, cut into ¼-inch dice
1 tablespoon dried oregano
3 radishes, thinly sliced
¼ head green cabbage, julienned
1 lime, thinly sliced

. . . .

The day before cooking the soup, rub the duck inside and out with the salt and oregano. Place the duck breast side down in a baking dish and try to prop up the neck area with a small cup or piece of crumpled aluminum foil so that the blood can drain out of the cavity. Cover loosely with plastic wrap or foil and refrigerate overnight.

The salsa can also be prepared a day ahead. Place the tomatillos in a blender with the water, cilantro, garlic, jalapeño, and salt. Blend on high speed until smooth. Use at once, or transfer to a bowl, cover, and refrigerate overnight.

Preheat the oven to 450°F. Transfer the duck to a rack set inside a roasting pan and roast for 1 hour, until the fat renders out of the skin and the skin turns golden brown and crispy. The meat should still be rare.

Drain some of the rendered fat into a large soup pot and place over medium heat. Add the tomatillo salsa, parsley, epazote, and *hoja santa* and fry for about 5 minutes to cook some of the acidity out of the tomatillos, stirring occasionally with a wooden spoon.

Carve the duck by cutting off the legs and wings and splitting the cavity in half lengthwise. Add the duck and bones to the pot and cover with the water. Add the hominy, bring to a boil, and then decrease the heat to medium. Simmer gently for about 1 hour, until the duck meat becomes nice and tender and starts falling off the bone. Remove the duck from the pot and continue simmering for 1 hour, until the hominy kernels begin to flower open.

Peel off and discard the duck skin and shred the meat from the bone. Return the duck meat to the pot and simmer for about 5 minutes to warm through. Adjust the seasoning with salt if necessary.

Set out separate bowls of the onion, oregano, radishes, cabbage, and lime so that each guest can add their own garnishes to their *pozole*. Ladle the hot soup into each bowl and serve at once.

Fideo is Mexican pasta known as a *sopa seca* or dried soup. It is considered a soup because it is cooked in broth, but most of the liquid is absorbed by the pasta. Frying the pasta gives it a nutty flavor and really helps bring out the chiles. It's important to use angel hair pasta nests rather than straight angel hair, as the air trapped in the pasta nests allow the noodles to fry more evenly.

This dish is seldom found in restaurants, even in Mexico, but always in people's homes. Because the pasta is unlike a lot of common Mexican cuisine, we had to put it on our Tacubaya menu and include it in this collection.

FIDEO

• MEXICAN PASTA WITH VEGETABLES AND CHILE •
• SERVES 4 •

1 to 2 cups canola oil

12 ounces dried angel hair pasta nests

½ white onion, cut into ¼-inch dice

2 celery stalks, cut into ¼-inch dice

2 carrots, cut into ¼-inch dice

About 1 teaspoon kosher salt

About 1 teaspoon freshly ground black pepper

1 jalapeño chile, minced

3 to 4 cups tomato sauce (page 203)

½ bunch cilantro, stemmed and chopped, for garnish

1 cup Cotija cheese, finely grated, for garnish

. . . .

Heat the oil in a skillet over high heat. Check to see that the oil is hot enough by submerging one pasta nest; the oil will bubble around the nest when it's ready. When the oil is hot, carefully add the pasta nests and cook, turning once, for about 30 seconds on each side, until lightly brown. Transfer the pasta to paper towels to drain.

Carefully drain off the hot oil, leaving 2 tablespoons in the skillet. Place over high heat and add the onion. Sauté for 4 to 5 minutes, until translucent. Add the celery and cook for about 3 minutes, or until it begins to lighten in color. Add the carrots, decrease the heat to medium-high, season with salt and pepper, and continue to sauté for about 5 minutes, or until the carrots are tender but firm. Add the jalapeño, toasted pasta, and 3 cups of the salsa. Bring to a boil, then decrease the heat to achieve a simmer.

Cook, stirring carefully, for 4 to 5 minutes, as the pasta begins to absorb the tomato liquid and naturally start to break apart. Continue to gently stir over low heat adding more tomato sauce as necessary, allowing the pasta to continue absorbing for about 3 minutes, or until it is firm to the bite.

To serve, divide the pasta among 4 bowls and top with a scant ladle of the tomato sauce. Sprinkle with the cilantro and Cotija cheese and serve at once; this dish does not hold well.

The first time I had *frijoles con todo* was at a tiny little taquería in Glen Ellen, California, that was run by a little cranky woman not much taller than a hobbit. At the time, I was living with my wife in nearby Santa Rosa, helping to fix up her mother's apartment in the evenings. During the day, I would travel fifty miles back and forth to Marshall Grounds Café in Sacramento. It often seemed that the only reprieve in my hectic schedule was the bowl of *frijoles con todo* from the grumpy little lady who knew that the path to a man's happiness starts at his mouth and leads to his belly.

We serve this hearty bean dish at lunch at Tacubaya, and it also makes a great vegetarian substitute for refried beans. If you keep a close eye on your beans while they're cooking and maintain the water level, it is not necessary to soak them prior to simmering. Keeping the correct water level is especially important for this dish since it's similar to *frijoles de olla*, a bean casserole served in its own juice.

FRIJOLES CON TODO

• PINTO BEANS WITH EVERYTHING •
• SERVES 4 •

2 cups pinto beans, picked over, rinsed,
    and drained
About 3 tablespoons kosher salt
2 avocados, cut into 3/4-inch dice
2 heirloom or vine-ripened tomatoes,
    cut into 1/3-inch dice
1/2 red onion, cut into 1/4-inch dice
1/4 pound queso Oaxaca, shredded
2 serrano chiles, minced
1/2 bunch cilantro, stemmed and chopped

. . . .

Place the beans in a heavy-duty saucepan and cover with cold water so that the waterline is about 3 inches over the beans. (The traditional method would be to cook the beans in an *olla* or earthenware pot, but any ceramic or heavy-duty stainless steel saucepan, preferably with a copper bottom, will do.)

Bring the beans to a boil over high heat, then decrease the heat to medium and add the salt. Simmer for 2 to 4 hours, stirring occasionally to ensure they aren't sticking on the bottom, until the beans are tender. Add more hot water from time to time to keep the beans fully submerged.

Stop adding water after 2 to 3 hours, when the beans seem close to becoming tender all the way through. The liquid at this point should be somewhat milky and cloudy and will start to thicken with the starch from the beans. You'll want the water to slowly reduce until it's just covering the beans when they're perfectly tender.

Adjust the seasoning with salt as necessary. Ladle the beans and broth into each bowl and top with healthy portions of the avocado, tomatoes, onion, cheese, chiles, and cilantro right before serving.

While this recipe is similar to Ceviche del Mercado (page 86), the flavor of its sauce is quite different due to the chilaca chiles. The richness of this sauce works equally well with fatty ahi tuna or light, salty, fresh-cooked Dungeness crab.

Follow the same method of preparation for the garnishes and tortilla chips as used in the Ceviche del Mercado recipe. Prepared tortilla chips can be substituted for either ceviche, although you'll be surprised at how large a difference little details such as frying your own tortillas will make. Try to obtain sushi-grade yellowtail from a reputable fishmonger and be sure to slice the tuna into strips no thicker than $\frac{1}{8}$ inch.

CEVICHE DE ATÚN

• LIME-CURED YELLOWTAIL WITH CHILACA CHILE VINAIGRETTE •
• SERVES 4 •

CHILACA CHILE VINAIGRETTE

1 dried chilaca (pasilla) chile

$\frac{1}{3}$ cup water

$\frac{1}{4}$ cup freshly squeezed lime juice
  (about 3 limes)

$\frac{1}{4}$ cup olive oil

1 clove garlic

About 2 teaspoons kosher salt

CEVICHE

$\frac{1}{2}$ pound sashimi-grade yellowtail tuna
  (or other seasonal fish)

$\frac{1}{4}$ cup freshly squeezed lime juice
  (about 3 limes)

Kosher salt

2 avocados, cut into $\frac{3}{4}$-inch dice

2 tomatoes, cut into $\frac{3}{4}$-inch dice

$\frac{1}{2}$ red onion, minced

$\frac{1}{2}$ bunch cilantro, stemmed and chopped

$\frac{1}{2}$ recipe homemade tortilla chips (page 145)

To prepare the vinaigrette, place a dry skillet over medium heat. Add the chile and toast for 2 to 3 minutes, pressing it into the pan and turning occasionally with tongs to prevent burning, until the skin begins to brown and the flesh starts to soften and collapse. While the chile is still hot, remove the stem and seeds and submerge in a bowl of hot water for 30 minutes to rehydrate. Drain the chile and transfer to a blender. Add the water, lime juice, olive oil, and garlic and purée on high speed until smooth. Cover and refrigerate until chilled. The vinaigrette can be held for up to 3 days.

For the final preparation, in a large bowl, toss the tuna with the lime juice and a few pinches of salt. Add the avocados, tomatoes, onion, cilantro, and about half of the chilaca vinaigrette and gently toss 2 to 3 times. Adjust the consistency and seasoning with more vinaigrette and salt if necessary and quickly toss a few more times so that everything is fully mixed. Spread the seafood mixture over a wide platter, line the edges with the fresh tortilla chips, and serve at once.

Although eating raw fish is believed to have originated along the west coast of South America, ceviche has long been an integral part of Mexican cuisine, particularly due to the miles of seafood-abundant coastline. The nature of this raw delicacy was forever changed when the Spanish brought with them the Arabic tradition of cooking with fruits.

In ceviche preparations, the citrus juices actually cook the raw fish to some extent—the citric acid reacts with the fish protein, tenderizing the fibers and altering the fish in both appearance and mouthfeel. The longer the fish is in contact with the citrus juice, the more it will cure, taking on more of a rubbery texture, so it is important to mix the ingredients immediately prior to serving. Cutting the fish into $1/8$-inch strips is also an integral part of quickly curing the seafood; anything thicker will not season or react properly. For those who may be a little squeamish about eating raw fish, cure it in the lime juice for about $1/2$ hour before adding the remaining ingredients; the texture will be much different, almost as if it has been cooked through.

As with any seafood, especially when served raw or cured, we recommend that you purchase only the freshest product—preferably sushi grade—from a reputable fishmonger. While this recipe calls for halibut, almost any fresh fish in season can be substituted.

CEVICHE DEL MERCADO

• LIME-CURED HALIBUT WITH AVOCADO AND TOMATILLO SALSA •
• SERVES 6 •

TOMATILLO SALSA
2 cups tomatillos (about $3/4$ pound)
$1/2$ cup water
$1/4$ bunch cilantro, stemmed
1 clove garlic
$1/2$ jalapeño chile
About $1/2$ teaspoon kosher salt

CEVICHE
$3/4$ pound fresh halibut (or other seasonal fish)
$1/4$ cup freshly squeezed lime juice (about 3 limes)
Kosher salt
2 avocados, cut into $3/4$-inch dice
2 tomatoes, cut into $3/4$-inch dice
2 jalapeño chiles, minced without seeds
$1/2$ red onion, minced
$1/2$ bunch cilantro, stemmed and chopped
$1/2$ recipe homemade tortilla chips (page 145)

To prepare the salsa, soak the tomatillos in cold water and then peel off the husks. Remove any dark spots with a paring knife and place in a blender. Add the water, cilantro, garlic, jalapeño, and salt and purée on high speed until smooth. Adjust the seasoning with salt if necessary and refrigerate until chilled. The salsa can be held for up to 2 days.

To prepare the fish, remove and discard any skin spots or bones with a sharp boning knife. Cut the fillets into 1 by ½-inch strips, then slice ⅛-inch thin slices on the bias from each strip.

For the final preparation, in a large bowl, toss the fish with the lime juice and a few pinches of salt. Add the avocados, tomatoes, jalapeño, onion, cilantro, and about half of the salsa and gently toss 2 to 3 times. Adjust the consistency and seasoning with more salsa and salt if necessary and quickly toss a few more times so that everything is fully mixed. Spread the seafood mixture on a wide platter, line the edges with the fresh tortilla chips, and serve at once.

We alternate between two types of shrimp tacos at Doña Tomás—sautéed and fried. They are very different in flavor and character, but both are quite simple, highlighting the fresh, delicious flavor of the seafood as opposed to drowning it out with intricate fruit salsas or heavy roasted vegetables.

We highly recommend using fresh 21/25—21 to 25 shrimp per pound—shrimp from a reputable fishmonger (if you don't really trust your fishmonger, use frozen shrimp). When cut in half, this size shrimp is ideally dispersed between pieces of sautéed onion, jalapeño, and garlic. Much like the flavor, the preparation and presentation of this dish are quick and simple.

TACOS DE CAMARONES AL MOJO DE AJO

• SAUTÉED SHRIMP TACOS •
• SERVES 4 •

¼ cup canola oil

1 white onion, sliced

1½ pounds shrimp (21/25 count), peeled, deveined, and split lengthwise

Kosher salt

3 tablespoons unsalted butter

1 jalapeño chile, thinly sliced

2 tablespoons chopped garlic

½ bunch Italian parsley, stemmed and chopped

16 (5-inch) fresh corn tortillas (see pages 35-37)

1 lime, cut into wedges

. . . .

Preheat a skillet or griddle over medium heat for the tortillas.

Heat a separate large sauté pan or skillet over high heat. Add the oil and onion and quickly stir 2 to 3 times. Immediately add the shrimp and a few pinches of salt and sauté for 1 to 1½ minutes, until the shrimp begin to turn red. Add the butter, jalapeño, and garlic and sauté for 1 minute as the

butter begins to melt and the garlic releases its aroma. Adjust the seasoning with salt if necessary and continue to stir for about 30 seconds; the whole cooking process for the shrimp should be no longer than 3 minutes. Stir in the parsley and remove the pan from the heat. The shrimp should be tender, the garlic aromatic, and the onions and jalapeños crisp to the bite.

Working in batches as necessary, warm both sides of the tortillas in the preheated skillet. Place them in stacks of 2 on individual plates or a platter, so that each taco ends up with a double layer of tortilla. Evenly divide the filling among the 8 stacks, and serve immediately with the lime wedges.

CLOCKWISE FROM TOP: TACO DE CAMARONES FRITOS (PAGES 90-91); TACO DE POLLO (PAGES 94-95); TACO DE CAMARONES AL MOJO DE AJO (THIS PAGE); TACO DE SALMÓN (PAGES 92-93).

The light, tempura-style batter in these tacos highlights the buttery flavor of the shrimp and is rounded out nicely by the chile de árbol aioli. Preparation and presentation are extremely simple when the aioli and batter are made ahead of time. At Tacubaya, we make a version of these tacos with snapper, a preparation that is similar to the traditional fried tacos often found in the coastal areas of Mexico.

TACOS DE CAMARONES FRITOS

• BATTER-FRIED SHRIMP TACOS WITH CHILE DE ÁRBOL AIOLI •
• SERVES 4 •

CHILE DE ÁRBOL AIOLI

1 dried chile de árbol
1 clove garlic
1 jalapeño chile
2 1/2 teaspoons cider vinegar
3 1/2 teaspoons granulated sugar
2 to 4 tablespoons water
1 egg yolk
3/4 cup canola oil
About 2 teaspoons kosher salt

BATTER

1 cup flour
1 cup water
1 egg

3 cups canola oil
2 pounds shrimp (21/25 count), peeled, deveined, and split lengthwise
Kosher salt

16 (5-inch) fresh corn tortillas (see pages 35–37)
1/4 bunch cilantro sprigs
1 lime, cut into 4 wedges

The aioli can be prepared well ahead of time. Place a dry skillet over medium heat. Add the chile and toast for about 1 minute, pressing it into the pan and turning occasionally with tongs to prevent burning, until lightly browned. While the chile is still hot, remove the stem and submerge in a bowl of hot water for 30 minutes to rehydrate. Drain the chile and transfer to a blender. Add the garlic, jalapeño, vinegar, sugar, and 2 to 3 tablespoons of water and purée for about 1 minute, until liquefied.

Add the yolk to the blender and turn the motor on low speed. Carefully remove the lid and add the oil in a slow, steady stream so it forms an emulsion with the yolk and the chile purée. If the mixture is too thick and won't blend well with the oil, add 1 to 2 more tablespoons of water, then resume adding the oil. If you add the oil too quickly the sauce will not emulsify and you'll have to start over.

The final aioli should have the consistency of thin mayonnaise with a speckled red color. Transfer to a bowl and stir in the 2 teaspoons salt, using more or less to taste. Cover and refrigerate until serving.

To prepare the batter, sift the flour into a large bowl. Add the water and egg and briskly whisk together until all the lumps have dissipated. Refrigerate the batter for about 30 minutes, then stir briefly before using.

Pour the oil into a skillet to a depth of ¾ inch and place over high heat for about 5 to 10 minutes (depending on your skillet and stove), until it reaches 350°F. Test the oil by dropping in a drip of batter; it should begin frying as soon as it hits the oil. Working in 3 batches, dredge the shrimp in the batter, then carefully place in the oil. Fry for 1½ to 2 minutes, until golden brown and crispy (the crispy texture is imperative as you don't want the shrimp to become soggy when tossed with the aioli). Transfer the shrimp to paper towels to drain.

Once all the shrimp are fried and drained, toss them with a few pinches of salt and about ¾ cup of the aioli to lightly coat. Adjust the consistency, heat, and flavor with more aioli if necessary.

Place a skillet or griddle over medium heat. Working in batches as necessary, warm both sides of the tortillas in the skillet. Place them in stacks of 2 on individual plates or a platter, so that each taco ends up with a double layer of tortilla. Evenly divide the shrimp among the 8 stacks. Top each taco with 4 to 5 cilantro sprigs and serve at once with the lime wedges.

Although mangos originated in Southeast Asia some four thousand years ago, Mexico's similar subtropical climate has been ideal for the fruit to prosper, making it a staple in a variety of traditional sweet and savory dishes. A ripe mango should gently yield to pressure and can be refrigerated for up to two weeks. The most flavorful tend to have a slightly yellow tinge and a fruity aroma emitting from the stem. The acidity and salt in this recipe help to macerate the mangos to a perfect consistency, so it's important not to start with fruit that is too firm or too soft.

The salsa is rounded out by the lime zest's pleasant residual acidity, which can't be achieved with lime juice alone, making it the ideal accompaniment for a perfectly seared oily fish (with the good omega-3 oils), like a fresh piece of salmon. We usually serve these tacos in the summer and fall, when the wild Pacific salmon return to the Bay Area from their long ocean journey and begin navigating their way back home toward the Sacramento and San Joaquin rivers.

TACOS DE SALMÓN CON SALSA MANGO

• ROASTED SALMON TACOS TOPPED WITH MANGO-SERRANO SALSA •
• SERVES 4 •

MANGO-SERRANO SALSA
1 large or 1½ medium mangos, ripe but firm,
    cut into ¾-inch cubes
2 tablespoons chopped cilantro
1 tablespoon minced red onion
¾ teaspoon finely chopped serrano chile
2¼ teaspoons freshly squeezed lime juice
Zest of ½ lime
4 pinches kosher salt
1 tablespoon simple syrup (page 204)

1½ pounds fresh salmon, skinned and boned
3 tablespoons canola oil
Kosher salt
1 tablespoon unsalted butter
16 to 20 (5-inch) fresh corn tortillas
    (see pages 35-37)
1 lime, cut into 4 wedges, for serving

To prepare the salsa, combine the mango, cilantro, onion, chile, lime juice, lime zest, salt, and simple syrup in a stainless steel bowl. Toss lightly with a large spoon just enough to coat the mango; avoid overmixing and breaking up the fruit. The salsa is best when used the same day it's made, but you can make it in advance and refrigerate for up to 2 hours, tossing again right before serving.

Slice the salmon as evenly as possible into 1 by 1½ by 3½-inch strips. (Or have your fishmonger do this, but make sure he doesn't cut it too thick or thin.)

Place a large sauté pan over high heat and add the oil. Season the fish with salt. When the oil is hot, add fish pieces one at a time, shaking the pan to prevent them from sticking. Once all the pieces have been strategically positioned, add the butter, decrease the heat to medium, and cook for 2 to 3 minutes, until the edges of the salmon start to brown. Gently flip the fish pieces with a spatula, being careful not to break them apart or spatter the grease, and cook for 1 to 2 minutes, until the second side is lightly browned. The second side will not form as nice a brown crust as the first side. Transfer the fish to a plate.

Place a skillet or griddle over medium heat. Working in batches as necessary, warm both sides of the tortillas in the skillet. Place them in stacks of 2 on individual plates or a platter, so that each taco ends up with a double layer of tortilla. Place a piece of salmon in the center of each stack with the more browned side up and top with ¼ cup of the salsa. Serve at once with the lime wedges.

Frying the tortillas gives these tacos a crispy outside and chewy inside, but be careful not to over-fry the shells or they'll be too hard. The fresh, light character of the tomato-cucumber salsa really balances this dish to make it a perfect lunch or party meal. Any extra salsa will enhance the flavor of grilled steak fishes such as halibut, swordfish, or sturgeon, or will go great with tortilla chips.

TACOS DE POLLO

• CRISPY CHICKEN TACOS WITH CHEESE AND TOMATO-CUCUMBER SALSA •
• SERVES 6 •

1¹⁄₂ pounds shredded chicken meat (from
    chicken broth recipe, see page 201)
¹⁄₄ pound Monterey Jack cheese, grated
¹⁄₄ pound mozzarella cheese, grated
Kosher salt

TOMATO-CUCUMBER SALSA
2 pounds tomatoes
¹⁄₄ cup chopped white onion
2 small cloves garlic
2 small jalapeño chiles, stemmed
3 tablespoons red wine vinegar
¹⁄₂ English cucumber, seeded
Kosher salt

3 cups canola oil
12 (5-inch) fresh corn tortillas
    (see pages 35-37)
¹⁄₂ bunch cilantro, stemmed and chopped

In a bowl, combine the chicken and cheeses, season with salt, and toss well.

The salsa can be prepared ahead of time. Place a saucepan filled about halfway with water over high heat and bring to a boil. Fill a large bowl with ice water. Stem the tomatoes and slash an X into the skin at the bottoms. Submerge the tomatoes in the boiling water for 30 seconds to loosen the skins, drain, and immediately plunge into the ice bath. Drain again, then peel off the skins. Cut the tomatoes in half crosswise and squeeze out as many of the seeds as possible.

Place the tomatoes, onion, garlic, jalapeños, and vinegar in a food processor. Pulse to a medium salsa consistency and transfer to a large bowl. Add the cucumber to the food processor, pulse until finely chopped (it won't chop evenly if you do it with the tomato), and add to the tomato salsa. Season with salt and mix well. This salsa can be covered and refrigerated for up to 3 days.

Place a large skillet or sauté pan over high heat and add 2 to 3 tablespoons of the oil. When the oil is hot, one at a time, add the tortillas and fry for 5 to 10 seconds on each side, until pliable (don't overfry or they'll become hard). Gently stack the tortillas on a plate and keep warm.

While the tortillas are still warm, fill each one with a scant $\frac{1}{2}$ cup of the chicken. Fold the tortilla in half over the filling, pushing the filling down to the bottom half of the pocket. Weave 2 toothpicks through the unfilled lip of the tortilla to hold the pocket closed. This step can be done a few hours ahead of time.

Place a skillet or deep sauté pan over high heat and pour in the remaining oil. When the oil is hot, fry the tacos 4 at a time for about 2 minutes, turning occasionally, until the filling heats up and the shells crisp slightly. Transfer to paper towels to drain. Remove the toothpicks, gently open the tacos, and fill with the salsa and cilantro. Serve at once.

December is a great month for us at Doña Tomás, because that's when the local Dungeness crab season kicks off—and we get to indulge in our crab taquitos, or "little tacos." It's not absolutely necessary to use Dungeness, but we like to take advantage of seasonal products, especially when they provide such a superior sweet buttery flavor. Serve the taquitos with rice and beans for a satisfying lunch entrée.

TAQUITOS DE JAIBA

• FRIED CRAB-STUFFED CORN TORTILLAS •
• SERVES 6 •

AVOCADO SALSA

1½ cups tomatillos (about ½ pound)
2 small or 1 large avocado, peeled and pitted
½ jalapeño chile
1 clove garlic
¼ bunch cilantro, stemmed
About 1 teaspoon kosher salt

FILLING

2 tablespoons canola oil
3 tablespoons unsalted butter
¾ cup peeled and finely chopped shallot
¾ cup finely chopped celery
About 1½ teaspoons kosher salt
1½ cups peeled and finely chopped carrot
Zest of 2 limes
1 teaspoon chile powder
1 pound crabmeat

18 (5-inch) fresh corn tortillas
    (see pages 35–37)
3 to 4 cups canola oil, for frying
Kosher salt
½ bunch cilantro, stemmed and chopped

. . . .

To prepare the salsa, soak the tomatillos in cold water for a few minutes, then peel off and discard the husks. Place the tomatillos in a blender with the avocados, jalapeño, garlic, cilantro, and salt. Blend on high speed until smooth and vibrant in color; it should be thicker than gravy but thinner than guacamole. Adjust the seasoning with salt as necessary.

To prepare the filling, heat the oil in a large sauté pan over high heat. When the oil is hot, add about 1 tablespoon of the butter and the shallots and sweat for about 2 minutes, until translucent. Decrease the heat as necessary to prevent browning. Add the celery and a few pinches of salt and sauté for about 3 minutes, until softened slightly. Add the carrot and cook for about 4 minutes, until fork-tender. Add the remaining 2 tablespoons butter, the lime zest, the chile powder, stirring until the butter is melted. Remove from the heat and allow to cool. Add the crab and stir gently, being careful not to break up any nice pieces of crab. Carefully adjust the seasoning as necessary (the crab will be naturally salty).

In a microwave, heat the tortillas on high for 30 to 45 seconds, until softened. Stack the tortillas on a plate and cover with a kitchen towel so they retain their heat and pliability.

Place about 3 tablespoons of the crab mixture in a line about one-third of the way from the bottom edge of each tortilla. Gently fold the bottom of the tortilla over the filling and roll up like a cigar. The cylinders should be a little over 1 inch in diameter. To keep the tortillas rolled up, place 3 of the rolls side by side and pierce through all of them with 2 evenly spaced wooden skewers. Spread the rolls out on the skewers to maintain 1 to 2 inches between them.

Place a large skillet over high heat and pour in the oil to a depth of $1\frac{1}{2}$ inches. Test the heat of the oil by gently submerging a set of skewered taquitos—the oil should start quickly bubbling on contact. (If the bubbles roar and spatter, the oil is too hot; if the bubbles are slow and lazy, it's not hot enough.) Working in batches, fry the taquitos for 2 to 3 minutes, until lightly browned. The taquitos should be fully submerged during cooking.

Transfer the taquitos to paper towels to drain and sprinkle lightly with salt while still hot. Unskewer the taquitos onto a platter, sprinkle with the cilantro, and serve at once with the avocado salsa.

Quesadillas are great appetizers for dinner parties and casual get-togethers, but also serve as a downright delicious lunch. We put this recipe on our menus at least once between April and June, when morels are in season and fresh asparagus is hitting the market. Dried morels have to be reconstituted in water, which dissipates a lot of their flavor. If you have to use dried, reconstitute them in the smallest amount of warm water possible to make the mushrooms pliable. Then sauté the mushrooms in butter, adding a few drops of water at a time until they are soft with a little structure to the bite. A more practical alternative would be to simply substitute any fresh, wild mushroom available.

Tortillas will also make a big difference to the quesadillas, kind of like the difference between serving a sandwich on homemade warm levain as opposed to a sliced store-bought loaf. Both may be good, but one definitely radiates a little more love. If you have to use shelf-stable (rather than fresh) tortillas, be sure to crisp them up well during the cooking process.

QUESADILLAS CON HONGOS, ESPÁRRAGOS, Y CREMA CON CHILE POBLANO

• QUESADILLA WITH MOREL MUSHROOMS, ASPARAGUS, GOAT CHEESE, AND POBLANO CREAM •

• SERVES 4 •

POBLANO CREAM

1 large poblano chile, toasted, peeled, stemmed, and seeded (see page 34)

1 cup milk

2 tablespoons canola oil

1$\frac{1}{2}$ tablespoons flour

$\frac{1}{2}$ tablespoon kosher salt

$\frac{1}{2}$ cup crema (page 198) or sour cream

$\frac{1}{4}$ cup heavy whipping cream

FILLING

1 tablespoon canola oil

1 shallot, minced

2 to 3 tablespoons unsalted butter

$\frac{1}{2}$ pound morels, coarsely chopped

Kosher salt

$\frac{1}{2}$ bunch asparagus, diagonally sliced $\frac{1}{8}$ inch thick

12 (5-inch) fresh corn tortillas (see pages 35–37)

5 ounces goat cheese

$\frac{1}{4}$ bunch cilantro, stemmed and chopped, for garnish

CONTINUED

To prepare the poblano cream, place the chile and milk in a blender and purée until smooth. Transfer to a saucepan over high heat and bring to a boil. In a separate small skillet, combine the oil and flour over low heat to make a roux. Stir constantly for about 10 minutes, until golden brown with a nutty aroma. Whisk the roux into the boiling milk mixture and decrease the heat to achieve a gentle simmer; the sauce should begin to thicken immediately. Simmer for about 20 minutes to cook out the flour taste, seasoning with salt as necessary. Remove from the heat and whisk in the crema and whipping cream. Adjust the seasoning with salt as necessary and keep warm.

To prepare the filling, place a large sauté pan over high heat and add the oil. Add the shallot and sauté for 3 to 4 minutes, until translucent. Add the butter and morels and decrease the heat to medium. Season with some salt and stir for 1 to 2 minutes, until the mushrooms are heated through. Add the asparagus and a little more butter if necessary and sauté for 2 to 3 minutes, until the asparagus is tender. Adjust the seasoning with salt as necessary.

Heat and lightly grease a griddle. Working in batches as necessary, place the tortillas on the griddle to warm. Place a small scoop of the filling on one half of each tortilla, sprinkle with goat cheese, and fold in half with a spatula. Brown the quesadillas for about 3 minutes on each side, until the cheese is melted and the outside is crisp. The quesadillas can be held warm in a 200°F oven as you finish the cooking process, but don't leave them in too long or they'll become tough.

To serve, arrange the quesadillas on plates or a platter, drizzle the centers with the poblano cream, and garnish with the cilantro. Serve warm.

Traditional quesadillas are rich but mellow—always filled with cheese such as *queso Oaxaca*, and often stuffed with such ingredients as *huitlacoche*, squash blossoms, or epazote. This quesadilla is an example of how we try to expand on this tradition at Doña Tomás by adding foods such as butternut squash, chanterelles, or porcinis, all of which are available in Mexico and complement the usual quesadilla ingredients but are rarely used in quesadillas.

QUESADILLAS CON HONGOS, EPAZOTE, Y SALSA TOMATILLO

• QUESADILLAS WITH PORCINI MUSHROOMS, EPAZOTE, AND TOMATILLO SAUCE •
• SERVES 4 •

TOMATILLO SAUCE
$1^1/_2$ cups tomatillos (about $^1/_2$ pound)
$^1/_2$ white onion, sliced
2 cloves garlic
$1^1/_2$ jalapeño chiles, stemmed and halved
$^1/_4$ cup cilantro leaves
Kosher salt

$^1/_2$ tablespoon canola oil
1 to 2 tablespoons unsalted butter
$^1/_2$ pound porcini mushrooms, cut into
    $^1/_8$-inch-thick pieces
1 to 2 teaspoons kosher salt
12 (5-inch) fresh corn tortillas
    (see pages 35–37)
$^1/_3$ pound queso Oaxaca, torn or shredded
$^1/_3$ bunch epazote, chopped
$^1/_4$ bunch cilantro, stemmed and
    chopped, for garnish

To make the sauce, preheat the oven to 350°F. Soak the tomatillos in cold water for a few minutes, then peel off and discard the husks. Dry the tomatillos and place them in a small baking dish with the onion, garlic, and jalapeños. Place in the oven to roast for 30 to 40 minutes, until all the ingredients are evenly browned. Transfer to a blender with the cilantro and a few pinches of salt and purée on high speed until smooth and thick.

Place a large sauté pan over high heat and add the oil and butter. When hot, add the mushrooms and sauté for about 10 minutes, until tender and nearly all the extruded liquid is reduced. Season with salt toward the end of the cooking process.

Heat and lightly grease a griddle. Working in batches as necessary, place the tortillas on the griddle to warm. Place a spoonful of mushrooms on one half of each tortilla, top with a sprinkle of cheese and epazote, and fold in half with a spatula. Cook for about 3 minutes on each side, until lightly browned, adding a dash more oil if the tortilla isn't browning evenly. The quesadillas can be held warm in a 200°F oven as you finish the cooking process, but don't leave them in too long or they'll become tough.

To serve, arrange the quesadillas on plates or a platter. Cover each with a spoonful of the tomatillo salsa, top with the cilantro, and serve at once.

Much like tacos, churros, and carne asada, *queso fundido* has become lost in culinary translation for most Americans. The typical Mexican restaurant version is a greasy, heavy puddle, a far cry from its original presentation. When made properly, *quesos fundidos* are a great appetizer or snack to be shared at parties. If you can't find *queso Oaxaca*, substitute a good-quality mozzarella and use a little less cream.

QUESO FUNDIDO CON POLLO

• BROILED OAXACA CHEESE WITH CHICKEN AND POBLANO CHILES •
• SERVES 4 FOR LUNCH OR 8 AS AN APPETIZER •

CREAM SAUCE
1½ cups heavy whipping cream
½ teaspoon ground allspice
Kosher salt

2 poblano chiles, toasted, peeled,
    stemmed, and seeded (see page 34)
3 tablespoons canola oil
1 white onion, cut into ½-inch slices
About ¾ pound shredded chicken (from
    chicken broth recipe; see page 201)
Kosher salt
½ pound queso Oaxaca, grated
¼ bunch cilantro, stemmed and
    chopped, for garnish
8 (5-inch) fresh corn tortillas, warmed
    (see pages 35–37)

To prepare the sauce, combine the cream, allspice, and salt in a small saucepan over high heat. Bring to a simmer, reduce heat to medium, and cook for 10 to 15 minutes, until reduced by one-third. Pass through a fine-mesh strainer to remove any film and set aside to cool. Cover and refrigerate if not using immediately.

Cut the chiles into ½ by 2-inch strips. Heat the oil in a large sauté pan over high heat. Add the onion and sauté for 3 to 5 minutes, until translucent, turning down the heat as necessary. Add the chile strips and chicken and gently stir until evenly mixed. Season with salt and remove from the heat.

Preheat the broiler. Evenly spread the chicken mixture in the bottom of an 8 by 10-inch, 2-inch-deep casserole dish. Spread the cream sauce on top and cover with the cheese.

Place the casserole under the broiler for 10 to 15 minutes, until all the ingredients melt together and the top is lightly browned. Sprinkle with the cilantro and serve at once, accompanied by the warm tortillas.

Since goat cheese is so delicate and won't hold up to much heat, it's hard to call this a traditional *queso fundido*. But the combination of ingredients is still quite scrumptious. The toasted pumpkin seeds add a warm nutty flavor that goes perfectly with the cheese's sharper notes. To get the sauce to the proper consistency, you'll need to finagle the amount of broth and the blending process.

QUESO DE CHIVA FUNDIDO CON PIPIÁN VERDE

• BROILED GOAT CHEESE WITH PUMPKIN SEED SAUCE •
• SERVES 4 FOR LUNCH OR 8 AS AN APPETIZER •

PUMPKIN SEED SAUCE

³/4 cup hulled pepitas

1 cup tomatillos

¹/2 bunch epazote, stemmed

¹/4 bunch cilantro, stemmed

¹/4 bunch parsley, stemmed

3 cloves garlic

¹/2 jalapeño chile

1 to 2 teaspoons kosher salt

1 to 2 cups chicken or vegetable broth
    (pages 201 and 202)

3 tablespoons canola oil

1 pound goat cheese

1 recipe homemade tortilla chips (page 145)

. . . .

To prepare the sauce, preheat the oven to 350°F. Spread the *pepitas* on a baking sheet and toast, stirring occasionally, for 10 to 15 minutes, until evenly browned. Soak the tomatillos in cold water for a few minutes, then peel off and discard the husks. Place the *pepitas*, tomatillos, epazote, cilantro, parsley, garlic, jalapeño, and salt in a blender.

Add 1 cup of the broth and blend on high speed until a slightly lumpy purée is achieved. Thin with another cup of broth if necessary to fully blend, but try to use as little broth as possible.

Place a large straight-sided skillet or frying pan over high heat and add the oil. When the oil is hot, add the sauce, stirring to prevent spattering. Decrease the heat to medium and simmer for about 1 hour, stirring frequently and adjusting the consistency with broth when it gets thick and starts to spatter. Check and adjust the seasoning with salt as necessary. Keep hot if using right away, or transfer to a container to cool. The sauce can be covered and refrigerated for 3 to 4 days.

Preheat the oven to 350°F. Separate the goat cheese into 4 portions, and form each into a 1-inch-thick patty (this thickness allows the patties to bake quickly and evenly). Place the patties in individual 4-inch ramekins and bake for 3 to 5 minutes, until the cheese softens but still holds its shape. Carefully remove from the oven and ladle the sauce over the cheese in a ¹/2-inch layer. Serve immediately with the tortilla chips.

Traditional preparation of enchiladas requires quickly frying fresh corn tortillas to make them pliable; submerging them in a sauce of puréed chiles (hence, *enchilar,* or to season with chiles); filling the tortilla with meat, vegetables, or cheese; and finally rolling, baking, topping, and serving, usually with beans and rice. Of course Americans have simplified this technique by initially microwaving rather than frying their store-bought tortillas.

We recommend using the traditional technique if assembling and eating right away, and the Americanized version when you need to assemble in advance for company. Regardless of the preparation and tortilla, it's important to work quickly when filling and rolling enchiladas so the tortillas stay soft. Serve the enchiladas with rice and beans.

ENCHILADAS DE VERDURAS

• ROASTED SWEET POTATO AND POBLANO CHILE ENCHILADAS WITH TOMATILLO AND JALAPEÑO SAUCE •

• SERVES 4 TO 6 •

1 poblano chile, toasted, peeled, stemmed,
    and seeded (see page 34)
3 to 4 tablespoons canola oil
1 white onion, cut into 1/4-inch dice
Kosher salt
2 large Jewel or Red Garnet sweet potatoes,
    cut into 1/2-inch dice (about 3 cups)
1 cup grated queso Oaxaca

TOMATILLO AND JALAPEÑO SAUCE
2 cups tomatillos (about 3/4 pound)
2 large cloves garlic
1 jalapeño chile, with seeds, stemmed and halved
1/2 white onion, sliced
About 1 teaspoon kosher salt
1 1/2 cups water or chicken broth (page 201)

12 (5-inch) fresh corn tortillas (see pages 35–37)
3/4 cup queso fresco

CONTINUED

Cut the chile into ½-inch cubes and place in a large bowl. Heat about 2 tablespoons of the oil in a large sauté pan over high heat. Add the onion and sauté for 3 to 5 minutes, until translucent and the edges have not yet started to caramelize. Season with salt and transfer to the bowl with the chile. In the same pan over high heat, add the remaining 2 tablespoons oil. When the oil is hot, add the sweet potatoes. Decrease the heat to medium and sauté for about 15 minutes, until tender in the center with slightly browned edges. Season with salt and add to the chile and onion. Allow to cool, then stir in the *queso Oaxaca*. The filling can be covered and refrigerated for up to 2 days, but should be brought to room temperature before using.

Soak the tomatillos in cold water for a few minutes, then peel off and discard the husks. Drain the tomatillos and place them in a stainless steel saucepan with the garlic, jalapeño, onion, salt, and just enough water to cover the ingredients. Place over high heat and bring to a boil. Decrease the heat to medium and simmer for about 8 minutes, until the tomatillos lose their vibrant green color and the garlic and onion become partially translucent and softened. Remove from the heat as soon as the skins of 1 or 2 tomatillos begin to split. Working in batches if necessary, transfer to a blender and purée on high speed until smooth. Adjust the seasoning with salt as necessary. Transfer to a bowl. The sauce can be covered and refrigerated for up to 2 days, but should be brought to room temperature before using.

Preheat the oven to 350°F. Heat and lightly grease a griddle. Working in batches as necessary, place the tortillas on the griddle to warm (the tortillas could also be microwaved for 30 to 60 seconds). One by one, dip the tortillas in the sauce and place them on a cutting board or clean work surface. Fill the center with 3 large tablespoonfuls of filling and roll into a cigar shape. Arrange the enchiladas tightly in a 9 by 13-inch baking dish with the seam side down (this size pan will fit a long row of 8 enchiladas and two perpedicular rows of 2 enchiladas each).

Spoon a light coating of the sauce over the top and sprinkle with the *queso fresco*. Cover the pan with aluminum foil and bake for 20 minutes, until hot. Remove the foil and bake for 10 minutes, until the cheese lightly browns. Ladle some of the sauce into the center of each plate. Divide the enchiladas among the plates and serve at once.

Sopes are a great way for newcomers to get accustomed to working with fresh masa because the dough is pressed thicker than a tortilla, making it easier to manipulate. This recipe also provides a good introduction to working with achiote paste, which is used in both the masa and the sauce. A tortilla press is not essential for making *sopes*, but it will definitely make the process easier and more consistent.

To adjust this lunch recipe to hors d'ouevres size for a dinner party, form the masa into smaller, 2-inch rounds. No matter what size you make them, the assembly of *sopes* is lots of hands-on fun.

SOPES CON CAMARONES

• CRISPY MASA CAKES TOPPED WITH SHRIMP, BLACK BEANS, ACHIOTE SALSA, AND AVOCADO •

• SERVES 4 TO 6 •

ACHIOTE SALSA

4 Roma tomatoes
5 cloves garlic
1 jalapeño chile
2 tablespoons canola oil
1½ cups diced white onion
1 teaspoon ground allspice
1 teaspoon dried oregano
Kosher salt
2 tablespoons achiote paste

MASA

2 pounds masa fina simple
4 tablespoons achiote paste (optional)
1 tablespoon kosher salt
3 cups canola oil, for frying

FILLING

2 tablespoons canola oil
1 pound shrimp (21/25 count), peeled,
    deveined, and split lengthwise
Kosher salt

1½ cups black bean purée, warmed
    (page 134)
1 avocado, peeled and sliced
½ bunch cilantro, stemmed and chopped
1 lime, cut into wedges

. . . .

To prepare the salsa, preheat the oven to 350°F. Place the tomatoes, garlic, and jalapeño in a roasting pan and bake, turning once, for about 45 minutes, until the skins begin to blacken and the centers become soft. Transfer the vegetables to a blender and place the roasting pan on the stove top over high heat. Add a few tablespoons of water and scrape the bottom of the pan with a wooden spoon to loosen the caramelized tomato bits. Lower heat to medium and simmer for 1 to 2 minutes, then pour this mixture into the blender.

Place a small sauté pan over medium heat and add the oil. When the oil is hot, add the onion and sauté for 3 to 5 minutes, until tender. Add the allspice, oregano, salt to taste, and achiote paste and stir a few times. Transfer the mixture to the blender with the roasted vegetables. Purée on high speed until a smooth paste forms with the consistency of thick tomato sauce. Adjust the seasoning with salt as necessary.

Place the masa in a stand mixer fitted with the paddle attachment. Add the achiote paste (if using) and salt and mix on medium speed until all the paste is incorporated; the consistency should be like soft cookie dough. Divide the masa into eight 2½-inch balls. Place a griddle or *comal* over medium-high heat and lightly grease the surface with oil or nonstick spray.

Line each side of a tortilla press with a piece of plastic bag. Place a ball of masa in the center of the press and close, applying pressure until the ball is about ⅛ inch thick and 4 inches round. Open the press and remove the plastic, gently evening the edges of the masa with your fingers if necessary. Lift the *sope* with your fingers into the palm of

your hand, peeling off the second sheet of plastic, then flip the *sope* directly onto the griddle. Sear it for 20 to 30 seconds. Cut the *sope* in half with a spatula and flip both pieces. Quickly crimp the edges of each piece to form a lip around the edges; the second side should also sear for 20 to 30 seconds. Remove the *sope* from the griddle and repeat with the remaining masa balls. The *sopes* can be held for up to a day at this point.

Pour the oil into a large skillet and place over high heat for 5 to 10 minutes (depending on your skillet and stove), until it reaches 350°F. When the oil is hot enough, turn the heat down to medium-high to maintain its temperature. Working in batches to keep them from sticking together in the oil, add the *sopes* and deep-fry for 4 to 5 minutes, until they become paler and form crusts. Transfer to paper towels to drain.

To prepare the filling, place a large sauté pan over high heat and add the 2 tablespoons oil. When the oil is hot, add the shrimp and sauté for 1 to 2 minutes, until they begin to turn bright red and are about halfway cooked. Add a pinch of salt and enough of the achiote salsa to generously coat the shrimp (you don't want them swimming). Bring to a simmer and cook for 2 minutes, until the shrimp are pink and opaque.

To serve, place 2 or 3 *sopes* crimped side up on each plate or arrange them on a serving platter. Spread a dollop of bean purée evenly on each *sope*. Cover the beans with 1 to 2 tablespoons of sautéed shrimp and salsa, garnish with a slice of avocado, add a tiny pinch of salt, and sprinkle with the cilantro. Serve at once with the lime wedges.

We're not sure which region *garnachas* originated from, or which came first, *garnachas* or *sopes,* but they seem to be most popular in the very southern regions of Mexico (Diana Kennedy's *The Essential Cuisines of Mexico* has a recipe from Yucatán). The version in nearby Belize and other parts of Central America is called *garnachas.* As you make your way north through Mexico, the identical dish is referred to as *sopes* (see pages 110–111). They're essentially the same thing, though *garnachas* are larger.

GARNACHAS CON NOPALES

• MASA CAKES WITH NOPALES, CRIMINI MUSHROOMS, BLACK BEANS, AND SALSA ROJA •

• SERVES 6 •

2 pounds masa fina simple

SALSA ROJA

4 tomatoes

1/2 white onion, sliced

2 jalapeño chiles, stemmed and halved but not seeded

2 dried mulato chiles

1 dried nuevo mexico chile

3/4 cup water

About 4 teaspoons kosher salt

FILLING

2 to 3 tablespoons canola oil

2 to 3 (3 by 6-inch) nopales, dethorned and cut into 1/2-inch diamonds

1/2 pound crimini mushrooms, sliced

Kosher salt

3 cups canola oil, for frying

2 cups black bean purée, warmed (page 134)

1/4 head green cabbage, sliced paper thin

1 cup crema (page 198) or sour cream

3/4 cup crumbled queso fresco

. . . .

Place a griddle or *comal* over medium-high heat and lightly grease the surface with oil or nonstick spray.

Divide the masa into twelve 2-inch balls. Line each side of a tortilla press with a piece of plastic bag. Place a ball of masa in the center of the press and close, applying pressure until the ball is about 1/8 inch thick and 4 inches round. Open the press and remove the plastic, gently evening the edges of the masa with your fingers if necessary. Transfer the *garnacha* to the hot griddle by lifting it to your palm, peeling off the second sheet of plastic, then flipping the *garnacha* directly onto the griddle. Sear it for 2 minutes, then flip with a spatula and cook for 1 minute to firm up the second side. Transfer the cake to a cutting board and depress the dough in the center and crimp the edges to form a lip. Place the cake back on the griddle for 20 to 30 seconds to brown the bottom if necessary. Remove the *garnacha* from the griddle and repeat with the remaining masa balls.

To make the salsa, preheat the oven to 350°F. Place the tomatoes, onion, and jalapeños on a baking sheet and roast for about 45 minutes, until the tomato skins blacken and the jalapeños and onion are browned.

Place a dry skillet over medium heat. Add the mulato and *nuevo mexico* chiles and toast for 3 to 4 minutes, pressing them into the pan and turning occasionally with tongs to prevent burning, until the skins begin to brown. While the chiles are still hot,

remove the stems and seeds and submerge in a bowl of hot water for 20 to 30 minutes to rehydrate. Drain and transfer to a blender. Add the ¾ cup water and purée on high speed until smooth. Add the roasted vegetables and purée on high speed until smooth. Season with salt and transfer to a bowl. The salsa can be covered and refrigerated for 2 to 3 days.

To prepare the filling, place a large sauté pan over high heat and add the oil. When the oil is hot, add the *nopales* and sauté for 2 to 3 minutes, until their color brightens and they begin to soften. Add the mushrooms and sauté for 5 to 7 minutes, until lightly wilted or lightly browned. Transfer the *nopales* and mushrooms to a bowl and add half of the salsa. Mix well, adding more salsa as needed until the vegetables are well coated. Adjust the seasoning with salt as necessary.

Pour the oil into a large skillet and place over high heat for 5 to 10 minutes (depending on your skillet and stove), until it reaches 350°F. Turn the heat down to medium-high to maintain its temperature. Working in batches as necessary to keep them from sticking together in the oil, add the *garnachas* and deep-fry for about 5 minutes, until lightly browned and crispy. Transfer to paper towels to drain.

To serve, arrange the *garnachas* crimped side up on individual plates or on a serving platter. Fill each with a spoonful of beans and a few spoonfuls of the *nopal*-mushroom mixture. Top each with a hearty pinch of the cabbage, 1 tablespoon of crema, and a sprinkle of cheese. Enjoy right away.

Pumpkins are found in a number of Mexican regional dishes. The flesh is used in soups and stews, plus tamale and enchilada fillings. The seeds are ground for moles and sauces or toasted with salt and chiles as a snack. The hulled seeds are green and more plump than the flat white seeds extracted raw from pumpkins. They can be found in Latino markets, health food stores, and online.

At Doña Tomás, we garnish our flan with pumpkin brittle, but it's also especially festive to munch on around the holidays. It is extremely important to work quickly through both the preparation and the cooling to achieve success with this recipe; it's helpful to have all of your equipment set out in advance.

DULCE DE CALABAZA

• PUMPKIN BRITTLE •
• SERVES 12 •

3/4 teaspoon baking soda
1/8 teaspoon kosher salt
1/2 cup corn syrup
1 cup granulated sugar
1 cup hulled pepitas (pumpkin seeds)
1/2 teaspoon pure vanilla extract
4 tablespoons unsalted butter

• •

In a small bowl, combine the baking soda and salt and mix well. Place the corn syrup and sugar in a sauté pan and bring to a boil over medium-high heat, whisking gently; try to avoid spattering the syrup up the sides of the pan. Checking constantly with a sugar thermometer, bring to 225°F. This should take about 7 to 10 minutes and the sugar should just begin to lightly color.

Add the pumpkin seeds and stir with a stainless steel spoon for 5 to 7 minutes, until the seeds begin to toast and the sugar turns amber. The temperature should now be 300°F. Quickly stir in the baking

soda and salt mixture. The brittle will foam up and begin to thicken and turn cloudy as soon as this mixture is added. Stir in the vanilla and butter and remove from the heat. Be very careful not to spatter anything on yourself since the mixture will be extremely hot and sticky.

Line a large baking sheet with a rubber baking mat or wax paper. Pour the mixture onto the baking sheet, spreading it out as much as possible. Allow to cool for about 15 seconds before flattening with a heat-resistant rubber spatula. Apply pressure from the middle of the pan outward, trying to press the brittle as thin as possible. The ideal thickness is the width of one pumpkin seed but it takes a little practice to achieve this. It is okay if the brittle is thicker, it will just be harder to break into pieces.

Let the brittle cool for about 1 hour. Break it into the desired size pieces, separate with wax paper, and store at room temperature in an airtight container for 2 to 3 days. After this, the brittle will begin to absorb moisture and become tacky.

LEFT TO RIGHT: DULCE DE CALABAZA (THIS PAGE)

AND POLVORONES (PAGE 116).

These nutty cookies are a great treat around the holidays, for special occasions, and, of course, as the name implies, for weddings. Be sure to check the date on any package of pecans that you buy, since the shelf-life should be no longer than 3 months. High quality pecans will average about 75 percent oil content, which will add more flavor to your cookies. The nut meat should appear plump and full, not dried and shriveled.

POLVORONES

- MEXICAN WEDDING COOKIES -
- MAKES 12 (2-INCH) COOKIES -

1 cup pecans, whole or pieces
1 cup cold unsalted butter
1 cup all-purpose flour
1 cup cake flour
1/4 cup granulated sugar
3/4 teaspoon pure vanilla extract
1/2 cup confectioners' sugar, for garnish

Preheat the oven to 325°F. Spread the pecans on a baking sheet and toast, stirring occasionally, for 3 to 5 minutes, until evenly browned. Watch the nuts carefully while they're in the oven since they can burn quickly. Remove from the oven and allow to cool completely. Maintain the oven temperature at 325°F. Transfer to a food processor fitted with the metal blade and grind into a fine powder.

Cut the butter into a few pieces. Sift the all-purpose and cake flours together. Place the butter, sugar, and vanilla in a stand mixer fitted with the paddle attachment. Mix on medium speed for 3 to 4 minutes, until smooth and creamy. Add the nut powder and mix in on low speed. Slowly add the flour and mix on medium speed until a stiff cookie dough is formed; be careful not to overmix.

Lightly grease a baking sheet with nonstick spray. Using a small ice cream scoop, scoop the dough onto the baking sheet, forming it into half-dome shapes about the size of golf balls. Bake for 25 to 30 minutes, until the cookies begin to lightly brown around the edges. Remove from oven, allow to cool, and dust with plenty of confectioners' sugar before serving.

These simple yet festive sugar cookies will brighten up any holiday table with their colorful display of decorative *grajea* (nonpareils, or little colored sugar dots). Be sure to adorn the cookies before baking or the balls won't stick. For an alternative sweet topping, you can substitute a mixture of 4 parts sugar to 1 part canela, or decorate half the cookies with nonpareils and half with the sugar mixture so your guests think you had to work twice as hard.

GALLETAS CON GRAJEA

• SUGAR COOKIES •
• MAKES 16 (2-INCH) COOKIES •

Scant 2²/₃ cups all-purpose flour

2 teaspoons cream of tartar

1 teaspoon baking soda

¼ teaspoon kosher salt

1 cup cold unsalted butter

1½ cups granulated sugar

2 eggs

4 ounces multicolored nonpareils **or**
   1 tablespoon ground canela mixed
   with ¼ cup granulated sugar

In a bowl, sift together the flour, cream of tartar, and baking soda, then add the salt. Cut the butter into several pieces. Place the butter and sugar in the bowl of a stand mixer fitted with the paddle attachment. Mix on high speed for 3 to 4 minutes, until smooth and creamy. Add the eggs and mix for 1 minute on medium speed, until incorporated. Add the dry ingredients and mix on low speed for about 2 minutes, until a stiff cookie dough is formed; be careful not to overmix.

Lightly grease 2 baking sheets with nonstick spray. Using an ice cream scoop or your hands, scoop golf ball–size balls of the dough onto the baking sheets, being careful not to overwork the dough. The cookies will spread to about 4 inches in diameter so leave plenty of space between them. Top each cookie with 1 teaspoon of the nonpareils or the sugar-canela mixture and place in the freezer for about 30 minutes, until firm.

Preheat the oven to 350°F. Bake the cookies for about 15 minutes, until lightly browned on the bottom and around the edges. Allow to cool before serving.

This traditional refreshment is enjoyed throughout Mexico and many parts of Europe. It can now be purchased in bottles and cans (even in the United States), but these versions don't capture the vibrant flavor of the freshly squeezed citrus.

The only trick to making a tasty *limonada* is balancing the sweetness and acidity, and perhaps having strong enough forearm strength to squeeze the limes if you don't have an electric juicer. The acidity of limes will fluctuate depending on the source and the season, but this recipe serves as a great guide for matching it with the correct sweetness level.

Without General Don Augusto Michel there would have been no Mexican Revolution and no such drink as the Michelada. Actually, the revolution probably still would've taken place, but we definitely would be deprived of this unique libation, which is not really a beer, not really a cocktail. Try one the next time you're on the fence about what to drink.

LIMONADA

• LIMEADE •

• MAKES ABOUT 1 QUART •

MICHELADA

• CHILE- AND LIME-SPICED BEER •

• SERVES 1 •

1 cup freshly squeezed lime juice
(from about 12 limes)
2 cups cold water
1/4 to 1/3 cup simple syrup (page 204)
1/3 to 1/2 cup mineral water

. . . .

Pour the lime juice into a large pitcher. Add the water and enough simple syrup to achieve your desired sweetness and stir well. Add enough mineral water to give the drink a nice fizz and serve immediately over ice.

Coarse salt
Juice of 1 lime
1 to 2 drops habanero hot sauce
1 dash Worcestershire sauce
1 pinch kosher salt
1 bottle Negro Modelo beer
1 lime slice, for garnish

. . . .

Salt the rim of a tall glass and fill with ice. Stir in the lime juice, hot sauce, Worcestershire sauce, and salt. Pour in the beer over ice and garnish with the lime. Serve. Drink. Enjoy.

We feature this watermelon sangría throughout the summer when the melons are at their freshest. The honey wine (mead) gives the drink an intense but light sweetness that is not at all cloying. Mead is indigenous to the northern regions of Europe, mostly drunk in areas where wine grapes couldn't be easily grown. It was gradually displaced as beers and ales became more popular and as imported wines became available. In some European cultures, a marriage was celebrated with a drink of this sweet nectar every day for an entire month after the ceremony, giving us what we refer to today as the honeymoon. When made with agave honey mead, watermelon, and citrus, the flavors of this sangría effortlessly evoke a Mexican honeymoon.

SANGRÍA SANDÍA
• FRESH WATERMELON SANGRIA •
• SERVES 1 •

FRESCA
Makes about 3 cups (enough for 4 to 6 drinks)

4 cups seedless watermelon chunks

1 cup simple syrup (page 204)

Juice of ½ lime

Juice of ½ lemon

1 tablespoon simple syrup

4 tablespoons agave mead (see page 14)

1 lime slice, for garnish

To prepare the fresca, combine the melon and simple syrup in a blender and purée until smooth. Place in the refrigerator for 1 hour, until chilled. The fresca will hold fresh for 1 day. Any leftovers make a great nonalcoholic breakfast drink, but should be reblended before serving.

Fill a pint glass with ice. Add the lime juice, lemon juice, simple syrup, mead, and a scant ½ cup of the fresca. Shake well and strain into a chilled tumbler filled with ice. Garnish with the lime and drink at once.

ENSALADAS Y BOTANAS

SALADS AND SIDES

This refreshing summer salad is the perfect accompaniment for spicy grilled meats and fish. The mangos' sweetness balances the heat of the chiles and the firm, juicy flesh provides a nice texture contrast to the crisp cabbage and jicama. The heat can be toned down by omitting the jalapeño seeds, although we feel the little bit of fire is what gives the salad much of its character.

ENSALADA DE MANGO

• SPICY MANGO SALAD •
• SERVES 4 TO 6 •

VINAIGRETTE
Zest of 1 lime
Juice of 3 limes (about 1/4 cup)
1 large shallot, minced
1/2 cup extra virgin olive oil
About 1/2 teaspoon kosher salt

1/8 head red cabbage, finely shredded
3/4 pound jicama, peeled and cut into 1/4 by
    2-inch matchsticks
1 jalapeño chile, with seeds, stemmed and chopped
1/2 red onion, minced (about 1/2 cup)
2 mangos, peeled, pitted, and cut into
    3/4-inch cubes
1 bunch cilantro, stemmed and chopped
Kosher salt

To prepare the vinaigrette, combine the lime zest, lime juice, and shallot in a small bowl. Gradually whisk in the olive oil to make an emulsion and season with a bit of salt.

Combine the cabbage, jicama, jalapeño, onion, mangos, and cilantro in a bowl. Add about half the vinaigrette and toss well, gradually adjusting the seasoning and amount of vinaigrette without causing the sauce to pool. Serve immediately.

A lot of the salads at Doña Tomás are designed as accompaniments to entrées rather than pre-dinner courses. This holds especially true in the summertime, when salads offer cool alternatives to hot vegetable dishes. Although the chayote is generally a tropical winter fruit, its year-round availability and crisp, mild flavor make it a wonderful match for sweet corn and summer cherry tomatoes.

ENSALADA DE CHAYOTE, ELOTE, Y TOMATES

• CHAYOTE, CORN, AND TOMATO SALAD WITH RED WINE VINAIGRETTE •
• SERVES 4 TO 6 •

VINAIGRETTE
¼ cup red wine vinegar
1 teaspoon chopped garlic
2 shallots, minced
½ cup extra-virgin olive oil
Kosher salt
1 pinch granulated sugar

2 chayotes
½ red onion
1 pint cherry tomatoes, halved,
    preferably Sweet 100s
Kernels from 2 ears fresh corn
1 bunch cilantro, stemmed and chopped
About 1 tablespoon kosher salt
About 1 teaspoon freshly ground
    black pepper

To prepare the vinaigrette, combine the vinegar, garlic, and shallots in a small bowl and mix well. Whisk in the oil, then adjust the seasoning with salt and sugar. The vinaigrette can be covered and refrigerated for 1 week.

Slice the chayotes lengthwise and cut into cubes about the same size as the corn kernels. Cut the onion in the same manner. Place the chayotes, onion, tomatoes, corn, and cilantro in a bowl and toss gently. Place in the refrigerator for 20 minutes, until chilled.

Add about half of the vinaigrette and the salt and pepper. Toss gently until the vegetables are well coated. Taste and adjust the amount of seasoning and vinaigrette accordingly, without causing the dressing to pool. Serve immediately. If the salad is tossed too far in advance (a few hours), the vegetables will break down and leave you with a soggy mess.

Roasting fresh beets in their skins, lathered with olive oil, and dosed with salt, creates a compact, sweet package completely unlike the canned vegetable that may haunt us from childhood. When purchasing fresh beets, select bunches with fresh green tops and firm, round globes no larger than baseballs; larger, elongated beets tend to be more fibrous. We like to serve this salad in the spring, usually around April or May, when beets reach their peak and blood oranges are still in season.

ENSALADA DE BETABEL

• ROASTED BEET SALAD WITH BLOOD ORANGES AND QUESO FRESCO •
• SERVES 6 •

4 fresh beets

2 tablespoons olive oil

⅛ cup kosher salt

3 blood oranges, peeled

Zest of 2 limes

Juice of 2 limes

1 shallot, chopped

¼ cup red wine vinegar

¾ cup extra-virgin olive oil

Freshly ground black pepper

½ pound queso fresco, pulled apart

Leaves from 2 to 3 bunches watercress

½ bunch cilantro, stemmed and
    chopped, for garnish

. . . .

Preheat the oven to 350°F. Slather the beets with the olive oil and salt and place on a small baking sheet. Cook on the center rack for about 1 hour, until the beets can easily be pierced with a knife. Allow to cool slightly, then wipe the skins off with a paper towel. Trim off the tops and the roots and cut into bite-sized wedges. The beets can be covered and refrigerated for up to 3 days.

Hold a peeled orange in your hand over a bowl and carefully cut the segments out of the membranes, letting the fruit and any juice fall into the bowl. Repeat with the remaining oranges.

Combine the lime zest, lime juice, shallot, and vinegar in a small bowl and mix well. Whisk in the extra-virgin olive oil. Season with salt and pepper to taste. The vinaigrette can be covered and refrigerated for a few days but should be re-whisked before using.

Place the beet wedges in a large bowl with the oranges and their juice, the cheese, and the watercress. Toss with enough of the vinaigrette to evenly coat and adjust the seasoning with salt and pepper if necessary. Divide the salad among 6 plates, garnish with the cilantro, and serve immediately.

Chicharrones and lard really give this dish a definitive regional flavor. Goat cheese may be more common in French cuisine, but Mexico certainly has its fair share of goats. The lard helps to tame the acidity of the vinegar and mellow the flavor of the cabbage. *Chicharrones* are simply fried pork skins, often eaten as a snack in Mexico but also used in prepared dishes. Both lard and *chicharrones* can easily be found at most Mexicatessens.

This is an elegant salad for formal dinner parties because most of the preparation can be done ahead of time, leaving the host to attend to the guests.

ENSALADA DE COL Y QUESO DE CHIVA

• WILTED CABBAGE, TOASTED PECANS, CHICHARRONES, AND CILANTRO
WITH BAKED GOAT CHEESE •

• SERVES 4 •

3/4 pound goat cheese

1/4 head red cabbage, finely shredded
(about 3 cups)

2 tablespoons red wine vinegar

1 to 2 teaspoons kosher salt

3/4 cup pecan pieces

1 cup chicharrones

1 tablespoon lard

1/3 bunch cilantro, stemmed and
chopped, for garnish

Lightly grease a baking sheet. Shape the cheese into 4 patties about ¾ inch thick, trying not to work them too much or the cheese will begin to melt. Place the patties on the prepared baking sheet, cover, and refrigerate for at least 30 minutes, until chilled.

In a bowl, combine the cabbage, vinegar, and salt and toss well. Cover and refrigerate for about 2 hours so the acidity begins to break down the cabbage fibers.

Preheat the oven to 325°F. Spread the pecans on a baking sheet and toast, stirring occasionally, for 3 to 5 minutes, until evenly browned. Watch the nuts carefully while they're in the oven since they can burn quickly. Remove from the oven and allow to cool completely, then coarsely chop. Increase the oven temperature to 425°F.

Place the goat cheese patties in the oven for about 3 minutes, until they begin to visibly soften. Be careful not to leave them in for too long or you will end up with puddles of cheese.

Chop the *chicharrones* to a similar size as the pecans. Place a large sauté pan over medium-high heat and heat the lard. Add the *chicharrones*, cabbage, and pecans and sauté for 3 to 5 minutes, until warmed through. Adjust the seasoning with salt as necessary.

Remove the goat cheese patties from the oven and quickly transfer with a spatula to a serving platter or individual plates. Spoon the cabbage mixture over the cheese patties, garnish with the cilantro, and serve at once.

Almost 95 percent of California's anchovy catch is used for bait fishing. The remaining 5 percent, however, makes for really good eating. Luckily for us, our fish purveyor often boasts fresh anchovies in his daily summer catch. Fresh anchovies should have an intact silver skin with few or no blemishes and a firm flesh that bounces back to the touch. Like all fresh fish, be sure they smell of the sea and don't have a strong fishy odor. Anchovies can be prepared a number of ways, but are best when cured or fried. Since they are most abundant during the summer months, we like to serve them lightly cured in lime with our favorite fresh heirloom tomatoes and a sprinkle of epazote for pungency.

The anchovies can be filleted a few hours ahead of time but should only be marinated 5 to 10 minutes before serving or the flesh will break down too much from the acid of the lime. This dish is essentially a ceviche, so fresh anchovies are of the utmost importance.

ENSALADA DE ANCHOA Y TOMATE

• ANCHOVY SALAD WITH HEIRLOOM TOMATOES AND LIME •
• SERVES 6 •

Juice of 3 limes
¼ cup extra-virgin olive oil
1 pound fresh anchovies
About 1 teaspoon kosher salt
Freshly cracked black pepper
2 pounds heirloom tomatoes,
    cut into ¼-inch slices
1 small jalapeño, stemmed and chopped
1 to 2 sprigs fresh epazote or arugula
    leaves, chopped

Combine the lime juice and olive oil in a bowl and mix well. Set aside.

To fillet the anchovies, gently remove the scales by running your thumbnail from the tail to the head along each side of the fish (too much pressure and you'll tear the skin). Do this under running cold water and the scales will easily wash away. Place the fish on a cutting board and with a sharp paring knife, slit the belly of each fish from head to tail. While rinsing the fish under running water, gently pull out the gills and entrails. Grab the spine from the underside of the fillets and gently pull it away towards the tail, trying to leave the head and the two fillets intact; this is rather like removing the string of

a snap pea. When done right, this technique yields two flat boneless fillets held together by the head. (You can also ask your fishmonger to scale, gut, and debone the anchovies, but he may charge you a bit extra.)

In a baking dish, arrange the anchovy fillets skin side down in one layer. Cover evenly with about three-quarters of the lime-oil mixture, being sure to douse all the fish. Lightly sprinkle with a layer of salt and pepper and refrigerate for 5 minutes. Flip the fillets so they're flesh side down and spoon the rest of the marinade evenly over the skins. Refrigerate for another 5 minutes, until the flesh is slightly lighter in color and the texture is a bit more firm.

Arrange the tomato slices on a platter or individual plates and sprinkle with a pinch of salt and pepper. Divide the fish evenly over the tomatoes, flesh side up, and pour the residual marinade into a bowl. Stir the jalapeño into the marinade, then drizzle the sauce over the fish. Sprinkle with the epazote and serve at once.

For many cultures, a meal without rice is not a meal at all, and we wholeheartedly agree. Our poblano and achiote rices (here and page 131) are both great sides to accompany any of our lunch and dinner entrées. They're simple to make and are nice alternatives to plain white rice.

ARROZ CON CHILE POBLANO

• POBLANO RICE •
• SERVES 4 TO 6 •

POBLANO MARINADE

1 cup tomatillos (about 6 ounces)
1 poblano chile, toasted, peeled,
    stemmed, and seeded (see page 34)
¼ bunch cilantro, stemmed
Kosher salt
Water

RICE

3 tablespoons canola oil
½ cup white onion, cut into ¼-inch dice
    (about ½ onion)
1½ cups medium- or long-grain white rice
2 teaspoons kosher salt

Soak the tomatillos in cold water for a few minutes, then peel off and discard the husks. Place the tomatillos, chile, cilantro, and a pinch of salt in a blender and purée until smooth. Add enough cold water to bring to 3 cups of liquid and quickly blend together.

Place a saucepan over high heat and add the oil. Add the onion, decrease the heat to medium, and sauté for 4 to 5 minutes, until translucent. Add the rice and continue to sauté for 5 to 7 minutes, until toasted to a light coffee color; this will enhance the flavor and keep the rice from clumping.

Add the marinade and salt and increase the heat to high. Bring to a boil then decrease the heat to medium. Cover and gently simmer for 30 to 40 minutes, until all the liquid is absorbed and the rice is tender. Fluff the rice with a fork and adjust the salt just before serving.

The annatto seed, known as achiote in Mexico, has a russet color and a bitter, earthy flavor when used properly in tamales, stews, and rice. The seeds grow inside heart-shaped pods on twenty-foot shrubs that can be found throughout South and Central America, the Caribbean, and parts of Mexico. This achiote marinade can also be used for hearty dishes such as whole grilled fish, *cochinita pibil* (a traditional Mexican pork dish), and meat stews. The paste has a strong earthy flavor that can be overpowering, so it must be used carefully.

ARROZ ACHIOTE

• ACHIOTE RICE •

• SERVES 4 TO 6 •

ACHIOTE MARINADE

Makes ¾ cup (enough for 3 batches of rice)

2 ounces achiote paste

½ cup freshly squeezed orange juice (or ¼ cup orange juice and ¼ cup lime juice)

2 tablespoons water

¼ teaspoon salt

¼ teaspoon ground cumin

¼ teaspoon freshly ground white pepper

1 pinch ground allspice

1 clove garlic, chopped

RICE

2 tablespoons canola oil

½ white onion, cut into ¼-inch dice

1½ cups medium- or long-grain white rice

2¾ cups water

2 to 3 teaspoons kosher salt

To prepare the marinade, combine all the ingredients in a blender and blend until well mixed. The marinade can be covered and refrigerated for up to 2 weeks, just be certain to remix with a whisk before using.

Place a saucepan over high heat and add the oil. When the oil is hot, add the onion, decrease the heat to medium, and sauté for 3 to 5 minutes, until translucent. Add the rice and continue to sauté for 5 to 7 minutes, until all the grains are well coated with oil and begin to slightly brown.

Add the water, salt, and ¼ cup of the marinade and increase the heat to high. Bring to a boil, then decrease the heat to medium. Cover and gently simmer for 30 to 40 minutes, until all the liquid is absorbed and the rice is tender. Fluff the rice with a fork before serving.

At Doña Tomás and Tacubaya, we begin each day by placing a massive eight-quart pot each of pinto and black beans on the stove. Beans are an integral staple of Mexican cuisine that transcends breakfast, lunch, and dinner, and their lingering aroma reminds many people of their favorite home-cooked meals. This recipe is an attempt to re-create the beloved dish that my grandpa would make every day of his adult life with his ancient wooden spoon, now retired to a place of honor in my kitchen.

Dried pinto beans have pinkish white flesh with brown speckles and a full-bodied, earthy flavor. They are easily found in any market or grocery store. Although virtually any type of bean can be used in this recipe, they all do have different flavors and cooking times. Smaller, darker beans usually take longer to cook and are much more distinctive in taste, often overshadowing the meatiness of the chorizo and lard. Keep in mind also that the longer beans are stored, the longer they'll take to cook, which is why you'll want to buy from a source that has good turnover.

Lard is traditionally used in refried beans, but we like to add chorizo as well; it contributes a nice salty spiciness that can't be achieved with lard alone. It's not necessary to soak the beans overnight to soften the skins, just simmer them gently, topping off the cooking liquid with hot water as needed. Failure to keep the beans completely submerged will result in uneven doneness, while cooking the beans over too high a flame will reduce the liquid too quickly and may lead to a scorched bottom.

FRIJOLES REFRITOS

· REFRIED PINTO BEANS ·
· MAKES ABOUT 6 CUPS ·

3 cups pinto beans, picked over, rinsed, and drained
1$\frac{1}{2}$ tablespoons salt
3 ounces chorizo
$\frac{1}{2}$ cup lard

. . . .

CONTINUED

Place the beans in a heavy-duty saucepan and cover with cold water so that the waterline is about 3 inches over the beans. (The traditional method would be to cook the beans in an *olla*, or earthenware pot, but any ceramic or heavy-duty stainless steel saucepan, preferably with a copper bottom, will do.) Bring the beans to a boil over high heat, then decrease the heat to medium and add the salt. Simmer uncovered for 2 to 4 hours, stirring occasionally to ensure they aren't sticking on the bottom, until the beans are tender. Add more hot water from time to time to keep the beans fully submerged. Drain the beans.

Place the chorizo in a large skillet over medium heat. Once the chorizo breaks down and starts to render, add the lard and allow it to come to heat. Add the beans. With a handheld masher, mash and incorporate the beans into the fat. Simmer for 5 to 7 minutes, stirring occasionally so the flavors have a chance to marry. Remove from the heat and cover the pan to keep warm until serving; the beans can be reheated over medium heat, but should be stirred to prevent scorching.

VARIATION: BLACK BEAN PURÉE

Substitute black beans for the pinto beans in the preceding recipe, following the cooking procedure until the beans are tender. Drain the beans and transfer them to a food processor and process until smooth. In a large skillet, heat 3 tablespoons of canola oil over high heat. Add half a minced onion, decrease the heat to medium, and sauté for 5 to 7 minutes, until translucent. Add the beans and fry for 2 to 3 minutes, stirring occasionally to marry the flavors. Adjust the seasoning with salt as necessary and top with grated Cotija cheese before serving.

This is a simple recipe for our favorite underestimated and usually poorly presented tuber. Many people are familiar with the nutty apple or pear sweetness of jicama, but have only been exposed to it within the confines of a crudités tray, often awaiting a pass through blue cheese or ranch dressing. Jicama is delicious enough to stand on its own without all that creaminess, but its porous texture absorbs flavors wonderfully, which makes this chile-lime salsa a divine accompaniment. This dish makes a great lunch salad or snack for just about any time of day.

JICAMA CON SALSA

• JICAMA WITH CHILE-LIME SALSA •
• SERVES 4 TO 6 •

CHILE-LIME SALSA
1 dried ancho chile
1 dried chile de árbol
½ to ¾ cup water
½ cup freshly squeezed lime juice
    (from about 6 limes)
1½ teaspoons chopped garlic
¼ cup extra virgin olive oil
Kosher salt

1 globe jicama, peeled and cut into
    ⅜ by 2-inch matchsticks

. . . .

Place a dry skillet over medium heat. Add the ancho chile and *chile de árbol* and toast for 1 to 3 minutes, pressing them into the pan and turning occasionally with tongs to prevent burning, until the skins brown slightly and the chiles begin to puff and become pliable. While the chiles are still hot, remove the stems and seeds and submerge in a bowl of hot water for 30 to 40 minutes to rehydrate. Drain the chiles and transfer to a blender. Add ½ cup of water and purée until smooth. Add the lime juice and garlic and mix on low speed. With the motor running, add the oil in a slow steady stream to form an emulsion. Adjust the seasoning with a few pinches of salt as necessary and thin with a splash of water if the flavor is too intense.

In a bowl, toss the jicama in enough salsa to lightly coat the pieces (you may only use about a quarter of the salsa) and serve immediately. Cover and refrigerate any remaining salsa for up to 2 weeks.

Grilled ears of corn are great summer sides, perfect for backyard barbecues. During grilling, place the corn on the outer parts of the grill and reserve the hotter center part for meat or fish. The corn will actually take a little longer than most meat or fish, so plan accordingly unless you want to eat it for dessert. At Doña Tomás, we don't grill the corn in its husk because the husk tends to burn, giving the corn an ashy flavor.

ELOTE A LA PARILLA

• GRILLED CORN WITH CHILE AND LIME •
• SERVES 4 •

4 ears yellow or white corn
4 to 6 tablespoons unsalted butter, melted
2 teaspoons kosher salt
1 teaspoon chile powder
1 lime, cut into wedges

Preheat the oven to 350°F. Preheat a gas grill to medium or prepare a moderate fire in a charcoal grill. Husk the corn and place in a baking dish. Bake for 10 to 15 minutes, just long enough to start drawing the moisture out of the kernels. (You can cook the corn completely on the grill, although it takes a lot of patience and a bit of practice to do so without completely charring it.)

Place the corn on the grill rack and cook for 5 to 10 minutes, rotating by a quarter turn every 3 to 4 minutes. When the kernels are tender and the edges are slightly browned, remove from grill and brush with the melted butter. Mix the salt and chile powder together in a small bowl and sprinkle evenly over the corn. Serve with the lime wedges.

A summer at Doña Tomás without corn pudding would be like trying to celebrate the Fourth of July without fireworks. We would have quite a few disappointed regulars if we didn't run this dish at least a few times between June and October. In the fall, we'll try other variations such as zucchini and scallions, or poblanos and green garlic, but the sweetness of white corn really sets the tone, and the fresh kernels help to elevate the texture to more of a soufflé than a pudding.

We try to use the sweeter, less starchy white corn whenever we can. Don't try this dish with canned or frozen corn kernels since they tend to be too watery and can drastically alter the texture of the pudding.

BUDÍN DE ELOTE

• CORN PUDDING •

• SERVES 6 TO 8 •

3 cups fresh corn kernels (from 3 ears of corn)
1 to 2 zucchinis, cut into ¼-inch dice (1½ cups)
⅓ cup all-purpose flour
3 eggs
3 egg yolks
3 cups heavy whipping cream
2 teaspoons kosher salt

. . . .

Preheat the oven to 375°F with a rack positioned in the center. (If using a convection oven, cook at 350°F.)

Place the corn and zucchini in a bowl and toss with the flour to evenly cover.

In a separate bowl, combine the eggs and egg yolks. Whisk briefly, then add the cream and salt and whisk until fully incorporated.

Butter a 9-inch shallow casserole dish. Evenly spread the corn and zucchini in the pan to ¾ to 1 inch thick (if the pudding is too thick it will end up wet and eggy in the center). Pour the batter over the vegetables. Bake, uncovered, for about 1 hour, until lightly browned on the top. It should feel like a firm pillow to the touch. Allow to cool for 10 to 15 minutes before serving.

VARIATIONS

Following the recipe above, substitute these vegetables or try your own combinations: 3 cups diced zucchini with 1 cup sliced scallions; 2 large roasted, seeded, and diced poblano chiles with ¾ cup minced green garlic; or 3 cups thinly sliced asparagus with 1 cup sliced green onion.

Sweet potatoes are a staple of Mexican cuisine and are believed to have originated in South America. The tuber grows on an annual vine that takes three to nine months to mature; it manages to grow well in the nutrient-depleted soil often found in South America and Mexico.

The term *yam* is often associated with Jewel or Red Garnet sweet potatoes (both soft, orange varieties), although a true yam is much larger, blander, and starchier. For this dish, we suggest using Beauregards—the lighter, sweeter, and most common variety of sweet potato that produces an ideal purée consistency. Of course Jewels, Red Garnets, or a blend may be substituted. All of the sweet potatoes we've used at Doña Tomás seem to increase in moisture as the winter progresses, so we adjust our milk and cream accordingly. We prefer a smoother purée so we use a food processor, but you can use a ricer or a handheld masher for a lumpier, more rustic texture.

CAMOTE

• MASHED SWEET POTATOES WITH CREAM AND PILONCILLO •
• SERVES 6 •

2 pounds sweet potatoes
1 cup heavy whipping cream
1¼ cups whole milk
1 to 3 ounces piloncillo
1½ tablespoons kosher salt

. . . .

Preheat the oven to 350°F. Place the sweet potatoes in a baking dish and bake for about 1 hour, until they are tender and can be easily pierced with a knife. Remove from the oven and allow to cool for 20 to 30 minutes. Peel the potatoes while they are still slightly warm.

Combine the cream, milk, and *piloncillo* in a small saucepan over medium-high heat. Bring to a boil, then decrease the heat to medium. Simmer gently for about 10 minutes, whisking occasionally, until the *piloncillo* is completely melted.

Place the sweet potatoes in a food processor and turn on the motor. Gradually ladle the cream mixture into the purée through the opening of the processor. Process just until the consistency is smooth and moist, stiff enough to form soft peaks, but loose enough to flatten smooth if the bowl of the food processor is shaken. Be careful not to blend the potatoes for too long or the texture will become gummy. Stir in the salt and adjust the seasoning to taste.

Serve right away or return to the saucepan and cover with aluminum foil until ready to serve. The purée reheats well in a foil-covered container in the oven; the sugar will caramelize more and enhance the flavor.

Vegetarians beware! This is a great vegetable side dish that we serve with everything from carne asada to salmon, but we don't try to pass it off as being vegetarian. The fresh lard is what gives it all the flavor. You can substitute leftover bacon fat if you prefer, or if you absolutely must go vegetarian, roast some garlic cloves in extra-virgin olive oil and use the flavored oil.

Do not rush the cooking of this dish—it has to go slowly or the beans won't brown evenly. Either Blue Lake green beans or French beans work nicely, though the latter do cook faster because they are so thin. Although not the most colorful preparation, what the beans lack in color they make up for in flavor.

EJOTES

• SLOW-COOKED GREEN BEANS •
• SERVES 4 •

1½ to 2 tablespoons lard or bacon fat
1 pound green beans, trimmed
Kosher salt
Freshly ground black pepper

. . . .

Place a wide sauté pan over low heat and add the lard. Allow the lard to heat slowly. Add the beans to the pan and spread into as even a layer as possible.

Maintaining the low heat, cook, stirring occasionally, for about 45 minutes, until the beans wilt and are evenly browned. The beans should be fairly soft but still maintain their shape. Season with salt and pepper and serve hot. This dish is sturdy and can be refrigerated for a few days.

Verdolagas is a mildly acidic green with a sweet, lemony flavor; they are usually available throughout the summer. In Mexico, *verdolagas* is typically served raw or cooked into stews. Though widely considered a weed, *verdolagas* used to be expensive and hard to find at Bay Area purveyors—even while, unbeknownst to me, it was competing for real estate with my own backyard calla lilies and tomato plants. Its growing popularity at farmers' markets (where it is sometimes referred to as *purslane*) and Latino markets has driven prices down to a reasonable level and now it seems to be turning up everywhere, even in cases of arugula or baby watercress. Try substituting this side for the standard spinach or sautéed greens. *Verdolagas* will discolor more than fresh spinach, but has a much longer holding capacity after being cooked.

VERDOLAGAS

• PURSLANE WITH TOMATOES AND GARLIC •
• SERVES 4 •

1 pound verdolagas (purslane)
2 tablespoons canola oil
3 cloves garlic, finely chopped
3 tomatoes, cut into ½-inch dice
Kosher salt
Freshly ground black pepper

Remove any of the larger, woody stems from the *verdolagas* and discard. Roughly chop the leaves and remaining stems into manageable 3-inch strips.

Place a large sauté pan over high heat and add the oil. Decrease the heat to medium and add the garlic. Lightly sauté for 15 to 20 seconds without browning. Add the tomatoes and sauté for 20 seconds. Add the chopped greens and cook for 3 to 7 minutes, until the leaves are wilted and the stems are tender. Season with salt and pepper and serve.

This toasty, spicy treat has become quite the popular bar snack at Doña Tomás. The concept is similar to the toasted pumpkin seeds often snacked on around Halloween, but since the hulls are removed, *pepitas* are easier to chew and digest. The chile and garlic enhance the flavor to the point of being addictive.

PEPITAS

• TOASTED PUMPKIN SEEDS WITH GARLIC AND CHILE DE ÁRBOL •
• MAKES 2 CUPS •

1 to 2 tablespoons canola oil
2 cups hulled pepitas
6 cloves garlic
6 chiles de árbol
1½ to 2 teaspoons kosher salt

Heat a large sauté pan over high heat and add the oil. When the oil is hot, add the *pepitas*, garlic cloves, and chiles; there should be enough oil to lightly coat everything. Decrease the heat to low and toss and stir the seeds for about 10 minutes, until they begin to puff and slightly brown. Bite into one or two seeds (be careful, they're hot!) to ensure that the skin has crisped (the skins will crisp a little more upon cooling as well). Sprinkle with salt and remove from the pan. Serve hot or at room temperature. The seeds can be covered and stored at room temperature for 3 to 5 days.

We originally didn't include this recipe and the one for chips (page 145), until we realized that a meal from this book without chips and salsa would be like a meal without bread, rice, or potatoes (depending on the culture). You can almost get away with burning the flan or dropping the tacos on the floor, because the first thing they'll remember is the extra love you put into the chips and salsa.

SALSA DE LA CASA

• CHILE DE ÁRBOL AND TOMATO SALSA •
• MAKES ABOUT 2 CUPS SALSA •

1½ pounds Early Girl or beefsteak tomatoes
3 to 4 cloves garlic
¼ white onion, sliced
1 dried pasilla de Oaxaca or chipotle chile
1 dried chile de árbol
¼ cup cold water
2 tablespoons apple cider vinegar
Kosher salt
1 tablespoon canola oil

. . . .

Preheat the oven to 400°F. Place the tomatoes, garlic, and onion on a baking sheet. Roast for about 20 minutes, until the edges of the garlic and onion brown and they become soft. Remove from the oven and transfer the garlic and onion to a bowl. Return the tomatoes to the oven and continue to roast for about 1½ hours, until the skins blacken. Transfer the tomatoes to the bowl with the garlic and onion and place the baking sheet on the stove top over medium heat. Add ½ cup water and scrape the bottom of the pan with a wooden spoon to loosen the caramelized tomato bits. Simmer for 1 to 2 minutes, then set aside in a separate bowl.

Place a dry skillet over medium heat. Add the pasilla chile and *chile de árbol* and toast for 1 to 3 minutes, pressing them into the pan and turning occasionally with tongs to prevent burning, until the skins are evenly charred and the chiles puff up. While the chiles are still hot, remove the stem and seeds from the pasilla and just the stem from the *chile de árbol*. Submerge in a bowl of hot water for 30 minutes to rehydrate. Drain the chiles, place in a blender with the ¼ cup water and vinegar and purée until smooth. Add the tomatoes, garlic, onion, and reserved cooking juices and purée until smooth. Season with salt to taste.

Place a saucepan over medium-low heat and add the 1 tablespoon oil. Add the purée and simmer gently, uncovered, for 30 minutes, stirring occasionally to combine the flavors. Remove from the heat and allow to cool to room temperature before serving.

It is, of course, much easier to buy a bag of chips, but compare your guests' responses when they taste these and we think you'll find the little bit of effort well worth it.

TOTOPOS

• FRESH TORTILLA CHIPS •
• MAKES 12 DOZEN CHIPS •

3 cups canola oil, for frying
24 (5-inch) fresh corn tortillas, cut into sixths
Kosher salt

. . . .

Pour the canola oil into a large skillet and place over high heat for 5 to 10 minutes (depending on your skillet and stove), until it reaches 350°F. Turn the heat down to medium-high to maintain its temperature. Cook the chips in 2 batches. Cook each batch for 3 to 4 minutes, submerging the chips with the end of a slotted spoon, until crispy. Carefully transfer the chips to paper towels to drain and season with salt while still hot.

CENA

DINNER

This recipe was inspired by a dish at Izote, Patricia Quintana's popular restaurant in the trendy neighborhood of Polanco in Mexico City. Quintana is noted for expanding the horizons of Mexican cuisine, which is perfectly shown in the combination of these ingredients. The concentrated heat and flavor of the ancho chiles are wonderfully balanced by the fattiness of the foie gras, the sweetness of the *piloncillo*, and the acidity of the vinegar. The dried anchos do not need to be toasted, but they should be soaked in the hot marinade for a good 1 to 2 hours to allow full rehydration and softening.

ANCHOS RELLENOS CON FOIE GRAS

• ANCHO CHILES STUFFED WITH FOIE GRAS •
• SERVES 8 AS AN APPETIZER •

MARINADE

5 cloves garlic, halved

1/2 teaspoon ground allspice

2 bay leaves

1 1/3 cups apple cider vinegar

2 cups water

1 (3-ounce) cone piloncillo

8 dried ancho chiles

1 pound foie gras

Kosher salt

Freshly ground black pepper

2 shallots, sliced

1/2 bunch cilantro,
    stemmed and chopped

To prepare the marinade, place the garlic, allspice, bay leaves, vinegar, water, and *piloncillo* in a stainless steel saucepan over high heat. Bring to a boil and whisk occasionally until the *piloncillo* dissolves. Remove from the heat and add the ancho chiles. Place a small plate within the pan to completely submerge the chiles. Leave at room temperature for at least 1 hour, until the chiles are fully rehydrated and are soft with a firm skin. The marinade can be covered and refrigerated for a few weeks; however, the chiles should be used within 2 days of being soaked.

Remove the chiles from the liquid and cut a 2-inch slit lengthwise into each, carefully cutting out the seedpod while trying to keep the stem intact. Reserve the marinade in the saucepan.

Clean any large veins from the underside of the foie gras and cut the lobe into 8 (2-ounce) pieces, about ¾ inch thick or the same size as the chiles. The lobe can be prepared a day in advance but wrap each piece with plastic wrap to prevent oxidation during refrigeration.

Preheat the oven to 350°F. Place a dry sauté pan over high heat. Season the foie gras with plenty of salt and pepper and place in the pan. Immediately lower the heat to medium-high and sear the foie gras, turning once, for about 1 minute, until evenly browned on both sides and plenty of fat has rendered off. Reserve the fat in the pan. Transfer the foie gras to a small baking sheet and place in the oven for no longer than 2 minutes, until soft but still firm to the touch.

Reheat the marinade over medium heat. Add the chiles and cook for about 3 minutes, just to warm through. With tongs, transfer the chiles to a cutting board. Gently stuff each chile with a piece of foie gras, being careful not to overextend the slit.

Remove all but 2 tablespoons of the rendered duck fat from the sauté pan (the rest can be saved to sauté mushrooms, spinach, and so on). Place the pan over high heat and add the shallots. Sauté for 30 seconds, just until translucent. Add 1½ cups of the marinade to deglaze the pan, scraping up any browned bits with a wooden spoon. Cook for 2 to 3 minutes, until reduced by one-third. Adjust the seasoning with salt as necessary and stir in the cilantro.

Arrange chiles on individual plates and cover each serving with a little of the hot pan sauce. Serve immediately.

Many of our sauces and fillings are versatile enough that they can be used for a number of different dishes. For example, with a few small changes, the filling for this relleno is very similar to that of Enchiladas de Verduras (page 106). This traditional relleno is usually stuffed with ground pork and dried fruits, but the full-bodied sweetness and starchy texture of the sweet potatoes are strong enough to stand up to the creamy walnut sauce. However, we do stay true to tradition by serving this dish only around Christmastime.

CHILES RELLENOS EN NOGADA

• ROASTED STUFFED POBLANO CHILES WITH CREAMY WALNUT SAUCE •
• SERVES 5 •

CREAMY WALNUT SAUCE
1/4 pound walnut pieces
About 1 cup milk
2 cups heavy whipping cream
Kosher salt

2 tablespoons canola oil
2 small onions, cut into 1/4-inch dice
   (about 2 cups)
Kosher salt
4 Jewel or Red Garnet sweet potatoes,
   cut into 1/2-inch dice (about 6 cups)
3/4 cup grated Cotija cheese
1/4 cup grated Monterey Jack cheese
10 large fresh poblano chiles, toasted,
   peeled, and seeded (see page 34)
Seeds of 1 pomegranate, for garnish
1/4 cup crema, for serving

. . . .

CONTINUED

Preheat the oven to 350°F. To prepare the sauce, place the walnuts on a baking sheet and toast in the oven for about 5 minutes, until they begin to lightly brown. Remove from the oven and place in a small bowl. Add the milk so that the walnuts are submerged. Place in the refrigerator to soak overnight, until soft.

Place the walnuts and milk in a blender and purée as fine as possible; it should be rather thick, like watered-down peanut butter. Add a little more milk if necessary to help with puréeing.

In a heavy stainless steel saucepan, bring the cream to a boil over medium-high heat. Decrease the heat to medium-low and simmer for 20 minutes, until the cream begins to thicken and is reduced by about one-third. Whisk the walnut purée into the cream and simmer for 2 to 3 minutes, stirring to prevent the nuts from sticking to the bottom. Season with salt to taste.

Place a large sauté pan over high heat and add 1 tablespoon of the oil. Add the onions, decrease the heat to medium-high, and cook for 3 to 5 minutes, until translucent and the edges just begin to brown. Season with salt and transfer to a bowl. Add the remaining 1 tablespoon oil to the same sauté pan and add the sweet potatoes. Cook for 10 to 15 minutes, until the edges begin to brown and the potatoes become tender. Season with salt and add to the bowl with the onion. Allow to cool slightly. Add the cheeses, toss well, and adjust the seasoning as necessary.

Prepare a relleno steamer as described on page 30. Stuff the filling into the roasted chiles, being careful not to overfill (tearing the pocket) or underfill (leaving the chile too empty and collapsible). Gently place the rellenos in the prepared steamer with the slits facing up. Cover the steamer and cook over medium heat for about 20 minutes, until the chiles are hot all the way through. Be certain to check and maintain the water level during cooking.

To serve, spoon a puddle of the sauce onto each of 5 plates. Carefully remove the rellenos from the steamer and arrange 2 on each plate with the slits facing down. Sprinkle with the pomegranate seeds, drizzle with crema, and serve.

After being introduced to Mexican cooking by Spanish settlers, cod became an extremely popular item in Mexico. It is often stuffed in rellenos or cooked with potatoes. *Tamales bacalao* are cod-and-potato tamales, truly unlike any other tamale you'll ever try. The saltiness of the cod and earthiness of the potatoes create a great filling that is perfect for the slightly sour pungency of the masa. The light tomato sauce rounds out the dish with just the right amount of acidity. It's important to soak the salt cod overnight, changing the water frequently in order to dilute the salinity. The banana leaf wrappers can be found frozen or refrigerated in most Asian and Latin American markets.

Serve as an appetizer or entrée and wrap any leftovers in plastic and freeze right in the banana leaves. They make great snacks after a quick reheat in the microwave or steamer.

TAMALES DE BACALAO

• SALT COD TAMALES •
• SERVES 6 •

1/2 pound salt cod

1 pound frozen banana leaves

2 bay leaves

2 cups whole milk

1 1/2 pounds russet potatoes,
    peeled and chopped

1/4 cup extra-virgin olive oil

1/2 tablespoon chopped garlic

2 tablespoons unsalted butter

1/2 cup heavy whipping cream

2 tablespoons freshly squeezed lemon juice

About 2 teaspoons kosher salt

1 pound masa fina simple

2 tablespoons canola oil

1 1/2 cups tomato sauce, warmed
    (page 203)

Place the salt cod in a bowl and cover with cold water. Refrigerate and soak overnight, draining and replenishing the water three or four times to dilute the salinity. Place the banana leaves in the refrigerator to defrost overnight.

Drain the cod and place it in a small saucepan with the bay leaves and milk. Bring to a boil over medium-high heat, then decrease the heat to achieve a simmer. Cook for 5 to 10 minutes, until the fillets are tender. Drain the cod and keep warm, discarding the liquid.

Place the potatoes in a separate saucepan and add cold water to cover. Bring to a boil over high heat, then decrease the heat to achieve a simmer. Cook for 20 to 30 minutes, until tender. Drain off the liquid then coarsely mash the potatoes with a handheld potato masher or fork.

In a small saucepan, heat the olive oil over medium heat and add the garlic. Sauté for 1 minute, then add the butter and cream and bring to a boil. Immediately add the cream mixture to the potatoes. Add the cod, lemon juice, and salt and mix into the potatoes with a fork, breaking apart the fish for a coarse, lumpy mash. Adjust the seasoning as necessary and set aside until the mix cools slightly, but is still warm.

Place the masa in a stand mixer fitted with the paddle attachment. Begin to mix on low speed. With the motor running on medium speed, gradually add the canola oil and aerate for about 10 minutes. The masa should be light in color and somewhat moist, but it shouldn't be wet and tacky.

Unfold the banana leaves and lay them out on the counter. Cut into at least twenty 6 by 6-inch squares, stacking neatly with the smoother side of the leaf up (you may want to cut a little extra depending on your level of expertise). Line both sides of a tortilla press with plastic bags (see pages 35–37).

Separate the masa into twelve 2-inch balls. Smooth side up, place a banana leaf square in the bottom of the lined tortilla press. Place a masa ball in the center of the leaf and press into a 5-inch tortilla (about $1\frac{1}{2}$ times the thickness of a normal tortilla). The top piece of plastic should easily pull away from the tortillas. When all the banana leaves are lined with a thick tortilla of masa, arrange them on a baking sheet and refrigerate for 10 minutes to make them easier to work with.

Prepare a tamale steamer as described on page 30 and line with wet towels. Place 2 tablespoons of the potato-cod filling in a horizontal line in the center of each tortilla. Fold the top edge of the masa over by one-third and bend the leaf back into place. Fold the bottom edge of the masa up by one-third and try to attach the two folds of masa together, then bend the leaf back into place. Fold the remaining two edges of the masa over to close the ends, then roll the banana leaf around the tamale. Don't worry about creating a perfect tamale since the masa will swell when cooked and will eventually work itself together.

Gently place the tamales in the prepared steamer, arranging them in a single layer with the seam side down to prevent unraveling. Cover the steamer and cook over low heat for 20 to 30 minutes, until the dough is cakey and stiff. Do not cook too long or the tamales will be dry and dense. Be certain to check and maintain the water level during cooking.

Carefully remove the tamales from the steamer and peel off the banana leaves. Arrange the tamales on a serving platter or individual plates. Top with the tomato sauce and serve immediately.

This *caserola* is similar to a lasagna, with layers of corn tortillas, sauce, cheese, and vegetables. You'll need to set aside some time for this dish since there are a number of steps involved, but if you get things prepared in advance, it's not difficult to assemble.

CASEROLA CON HUITLACOCHE

• TORTILLA CASSEROLE WITH HUITLACOCHE, CHARD, CORN, AND CHEESE •
• SERVES 6 •

3 tablespoons canola oil

3/4 cup diced white onion

Kernels from 3 ears fresh corn

1/2 pound huitlacoche

Kosher salt

1 bunch Swiss chard, stemmed and cut into
    1/2 by 2-inch strips

6 poblano chiles, toasted, peeled, seeded,
    and cut into 1-inch pieces (see page 34)

6 ounces Monterey Jack cheese, grated

6 ounces mozzarella cheese, grated

18 to 20 (5-inch) fresh corn tortillas
    (see pages 35–37)

2 to 3 cups tomato sauce (page 203)

Place a large sauté pan over medium-high heat and add 1 tablespoon of the oil. Add the onion and sauté for 3 to 5 minutes, until tender and translucent. Add 1 more tablespoon of the oil to the pan and add the corn. Sauté for 2 to 3 minutes, until tender, and add the huitlacoche, sautéing for another 3 to 4 minutes, until tender. Transfer the onion, corn, and huitlacoche to a bowl and season with salt. Heat another tablespoon of oil in the pan and sauté the chard for 3 to 5 minutes, until tender and wilted. Transfer the chard to the bowl with the other vegetables, add the chiles, and adjust the seasoning with salt as necessary.

Preheat the oven to 350°F. Mix the cheeses together in a bowl.

Place a lightly greased skillet or *comal* over high heat. Lightly grease the tortillas with canola oil or nonstick spray to soften them. Place the tortillas in the skillet and warm each side for 30 seconds, until pliable and hot but not browned. Stack the tortillas on a plate to keep warm.

Lightly oil a 9 by 13-inch baking dish and drizzle the bottom with 1/2 cup of the tomato sauce. Spread the sauce evenly and cover with a single layer of the tortillas, overlapping as little as possible (you may need to cut most of the tortillas in half) and lining the flat side of the tortilla up with the flat edges of the pan. Once the edges of the *caserola* have been established it takes about three tortillas to cover the center. Add another 1/2 cup of the sauce and spread thin with the back of a ladle. Evenly sprinkle on one-third of the cheese mixture and then half of the vegetable mixture. Top with another layer of tortillas. Repeat the layers of sauce, cheese, and vegetables (using up all of the vegetables) and top with a final layer of tortillas. Top the last layer of tortillas with another 1/2 cup of the sauce and the remaining cheese (you should still have about 1 cup of sauce).

Bake, uncovered, for 15 to 20 minutes, until the top begins to brown and all the cheese is melted. Remove from the oven and allow to rest for about 5 minutes before cutting. While the *caserola* is baking, gently bring the remaining tomato sauce to a boil. To serve, ladle some sauce onto each plate and top with a thick piece of casserole.

Both the method and the ingredients (especially the pork) contribute to the nice, moist texture of our meatballs. The crispy outside and tender inside are achieved by steaming and then lightly panfrying the meatballs before adding them to the soup. With this traditional meatball dish, we often change the base of the soup to reflect the season—tomato in the summer and carrot in the winter.

For the breadcrumbs, we use *talera* or *bolillo* rolls—crusty, sweet breads often used for *tortas*—which can be found in most Mexican bakeries. Any soft, sweet, crusty baguette will suffice as long as you can get about 1½ cups of large, coarse breadcrumbs out of it.

ALBÓNDIGAS

• BEEF AND PORK MEATBALLS IN CARROT SOUP •
• SERVES 5 •

CARROT SOUP

Makes about 4 cups

3 tablespoons canola oil

1 white onion, chopped

1 pound carrots, chopped

1½ serrano chiles, chopped

3 to 4 cups chicken broth (page 201)

1 cup heavy whipping cream

Kosher salt

¼ bunch fresh parsley or cilantro, stemmed and chopped, for garnish

MEATBALLS

Makes 15 (2½-inch) meatballs

⅓ loaf sweet baguette, stale or dried in the oven

½ cup whole milk

7 tablespoons canola oil

2 cups minced white onion

Kosher salt

2 ½ pounds ground beef

¾ pound ground pork

3 eggs

½ cup crumbled Cotija cheese

¼ bunch fresh parsley, chopped

½ bunch fresh marjoram

½ tablespoon cumin powder

CONTINUED

To prepare the soup, place a saucepan over high heat and add the oil. When the oil is hot, add the onion and sauté for 3 to 5 minutes, until translucent. Decrease the heat to medium and add the carrots and chiles. Cook for 5 to 7 minutes to sweat the carrots and bring out some of the sugars. Add the broth and bring to a boil, then decrease the heat to medium. Simmer for 30 to 40 minutes, until the flavors come together and the carrots are tender.

Transfer the soup to a blender and purée until smooth. Return the soup to the pot over medium heat. Whisk in the cream, season with salt to taste, and adjust the consistency with broth or water as necessary. Simmer for 10 to 15 minutes to help the flavors come together. Keep warm. (If making the soup ahead of time, don't add the cream until reheating to prevent scorching and spoiling.)

To prepare the meatballs, place the bread in a food processor and pulse to form large crumbs, ¼ to ½ inch in size. Place the crumbs and milk in a bowl and allow to soak at room temperature.

Place a large sauté pan over high heat and add 3 tablespoons of the oil. Add the onion and sauté for 3 to 5 minutes, until translucent. Add a few pinches of salt during cooking to bring out the flavor and aroma. Adjust the heat as necessary to prevent browning. Allow to cool slightly.

Combine the beef, pork, eggs, cheese, parsley, marjoram, cumin, and 1 tablespoon of salt in a large bowl. Mix by hand for 1 to 2 minutes, until the eggs are completely worked into the meat. Add the onions and soaked breadcrumbs and mix for 30 seconds, until everything is incorporated. The meat should be slightly tacky but dry enough to be shapeable. If too sticky, add a few more breadcrumbs, if too dry, add a splash of milk. If you like, you can test the flavor of the meatballs: before forming the mixture into balls, pan-sear a small patty, taste, and adjust the seasoning as necessary.

To make the meatballs, prepare a steamer as described on page 30 for rellenos and tamales. Form the meat mixture into balls a little bit smaller than a baseball. Arrange the balls in the steamer. Cover the steamer and cook over medium heat for 15 to 30 minutes, until the meatballs are no longer pink in the center, and reach an internal temperature of 165°F. Be certain to check and maintain the water level during cooking. Carefully remove the meatballs from the steamer.

Place a large skillet or sauté pan over high heat and add the remaining 4 tablespoons oil. When the oil is hot, add the meatballs and fry, gently turning, for 10 to 12 minutes, until the meat browns and forms a thin crust. Divide the meatballs among soup bowls, cover with a few ladles of hot soup, and garnish with a pinch of the parsley. Serve at once.

Mushrooms serve as an integral part of Mexican cuisine, especially in the high mountain region of Tlaxcala, where there is said to be more than seventy species of edible fungi growing beneath the towering pines. We prefer chanterelles and hen of the woods for this preparation, but any flavorful, woody mushroom can be substituted. A blend of criminis and shiitakes has the best chance of standing up to the strong, smoky flavor of the chipotles.

A *carnicería* (Latin meat market) or decent butcher should be able to provide you with a beef bavette—a thin slice from the short loin that is cut against the grain. A simple *ranchera* or flank steak can also be used. Avoid cuts such as the *bolla*, which is from the leg and is too tough due to the lack of fat. Regardless of the cut selection, slicing the steak as thin as possible and against the grain are paramount for this recipe. Since we often enjoy this dish in the fall, we like to serve it with a watercress salad and mashed sweet potatoes (Camote, page 140).

CARNE ASADA CON CREMA DE CLAVITOS

• BEEF WITH WILD MUSHROOMS AND CREAMY CHIPOTLE SAUCE •
• SERVES 6 •

SAUCE

3 chipotle chiles in adobo sauce

1 cup whole milk

1 cup heavy whipping cream

2 tablespoons canola oil

1½ tablespoons all-purpose flour

Kosher salt

½ cup crema (page 198) or sour cream

¼ cup canola oil

8 ounces hen of the woods mushrooms

8 ounces chanterelle mushrooms

Kosher salt

3 (¾-pound) beef bavettes, trimmed of sinews

Freshly cracked black pepper

. . . .

CONTINUED

To prepare the sauce, combine the chipotles and milk in a blender and process on high speed for 30 seconds, until the chiles are completely incorporated into the milk. Transfer to a saucepan and add the cream. Bring to a boil over high heat and then decrease the heat to achieve a simmer.

Heat the oil in a small sauté pan over medium-low heat. Add the flour and cook, stirring frequently with a wooden spoon, for about 10 minutes, until amber colored with the aroma of toasted hazelnuts. Whisk this roux into the chile mixture and simmer gently over medium heat for 10 to 15 minutes, until the sauce thickens. Season to taste with salt and remove from the heat. Whisk in the crema, which will thicken the sauce and round out the rich, velvety texture. Allow to cool. Use immediately or cover and refrigerate for up to 3 days.

Preheat a gas grill to medium-high or prepare a hot fire in a charcoal grill. Place a large sauté pan with deep sides over high heat and add 2 tablespoons of the oil. When the oil is hot, add the mushrooms and sauté for 5 to 7 minutes, until they begin to wilt. Season with salt during cooking. The mushrooms can soak up a lot of salt and oil, so be sure not to oversaturate them. Add the cream sauce and gently bring to a boil over medium-high heat, adjusting the seasoning with salt as necessary. Keep warm.

Rub the meat with some canola oil and season both sides with salt and cracked pepper. Place the meat on the grill rack and cook, flipping about every 2 minutes, for 5 to 10 minutes for medium rare. Allow the meat to rest on a platter for about 5 minutes before slicing and serving. Slice the meat against the grain as thinly as possible and arrange on a serving platter or individual plates. Ladle the mushroom sauce over the beef and serve at once.

Traditionally, *barbacoa* is made with turkey, lamb, or goat. The whole animal is butchered, rubbed with a chile marinade, arranged in *ollas* (large clay pots), layered with agave or banana leaves, and slow roasted for up to twenty-four hours over a wood fire in a sunken barbecue pit, often covered with a mound of earth. Outside of having to dig up a considerable piece of the backyard and finding a clay pot large enough to fit a lamb (or a lamb small enough to fit in a clay pot), we've come up with a viable indoor alternative that retains quite a bit of integrity for such a traditional dish. Just as with the original version, in our preparation, the flavor of the chiles and banana leaves absorb into the meat during the long, slow braise and the meat has plenty of time to get nice and tender. You'll want to serve this dish with plenty of rice and corn tortillas for sopping up the juices.

This is a great dish for entertaining since the meat should be placed in the oven 4 to 5 hours prior to your guests' arrival, leaving very little for last-minute preparation. At least you won't have to listen to your neighbors ask when you'll be filling in the unsightly charred hole you've left in your backyard.

BARBACOA DE BORREGO

• LAMB SHOULDER SLOW ROASTED IN BANANA LEAVES WITH
ANCHO-GUAJILLO CHILE SAUCE •
• SERVES 6 TO 8 •

ANCHO-GUAJILLO CHILE SAUCE
6 dried ancho chiles
6 dried guajillo chiles
5 tablespoons canola oil
2 white onions, coarsely chopped
5 cloves garlic
1 tablespoon dried oregano
1 quart water
Kosher salt

3 pounds lamb shoulder, cut into 3-inch pieces
Kosher salt
Freshly ground black pepper
¼ cup canola oil
2 to 3 large banana leaves
1 white onion, coarsely chopped
1 carrot, coarsely chopped
¼ cup mezcal
7 whole cloves
7 whole allspice berries
3 to 4 cups chicken broth (page 201)

To make the sauce, place a dry skillet over medium heat. Add the ancho and guajillo chiles and toast for 2 to 3 minutes, pressing them into the pan and turning occasionally with tongs to prevent burning, until the skins begin to brown and the chiles become soft and flexible and give off their spicy aroma. While the chiles are still hot, remove the stems and seeds and submerge in a bowl of hot water for about 30 minutes to rehydrate.

Place a sauté pan over high heat and add 3 tablespoons of the oil. Add the onions and sauté, stirring occasionally, for 3 to 4 minutes, until softened. Decrease the heat as necessary to prevent browning. Transfer the onions to a blender. Heat the remaining 2 tablespoons oil in the pan over low heat and add the garlic. Slowly roast for 7 to 10 minutes, until lightly browned. Transfer the garlic without oil to the blender with the onion.

Drain the chiles and add to the blender with the oregano, water, and salt to taste. Purée on high speed until smooth and incorporated. Adjust the seasoning with salt as necessary. Use immediately or cover and refrigerate for up to 1 week; be sure to whisk well before using.

Season the lamb well with salt and pepper. Heat a 12-inch braising pan over high heat and add the oil. Place the meat in the braising pan in an even layer and sear for 3 to 5 minutes, until caramelized on the bottom. Decrease the heat to medium-high and turn the meat over. Cook the second side for 7 to 10 minutes, until browned. Remove the meat from the pan and wipe out any residual oil. Allow the pan to cool for 5 minutes.

Preheat the oven to 300°F. Line the braising pan as thoroughly as possible with a large banana leaf (you may need to cut or tear the leaf to make it conform to the pan). Cover the leaf with the onion and carrot and evenly layer the meat over the vegetables. Sprinkle the meat with the mezcal, cloves, and allspice. Add about 1 quart of the sauce so that the lamb is half submerged. Top with 3 or more cups of the chicken broth, so the lamb is fully submerged. Cover the whole assembly with another layer of banana leaf, then cover the pan with a lid or aluminum foil. Roast for 3 to 4 hours, until the meat is tender, piercing with a metal skewer or small knife to check for doneness.

Transfer the entire braising pan to the stove top. Remove the upper layer of banana leaf and discard. With tongs, gently remove the pieces of lamb and set aside on a serving platter. Remove the bottom and side pieces of banana leaf and discard.

Heat the braising liquid over high heat. Skim off the layer of floating fat and cook for 20 to 30 minutes, until reduced by about one-third and the sauce begins to thicken. When the proper consistency is achieved, taste and adjust the seasoning with salt and pepper as necessary. Generously spoon the sauce over the meat just before serving.

Agridulce means "bittersweet" in Spanish, and although mole for many denotes a blend of spicy peppers and bitter herbs doused with a few ladles of sweet melted chocolate, this recipe is a far cry from the norm. As a matter of fact, it doesn't even have a hint of chocolate. The guajillo chiles provide the bitterness and heat, the sweet and sour are derived from the citrus and pineapple, and all the predominant flavors are well balanced with just the right blend of spices.

Mole is a dish often prepared for celebrations, and one that varies from region to region. The word is derived from the Nahuatl word *molli*—which means either "mixture" or "sauce" depending on the translation.

Most moles can be somewhat time-consuming to make (which may be why they're often reserved for special occasions), simply due to the long list of ingredients. The cooking methods, however, are quite basic and the rewards will not go unnoticed. The nice thing about moles is that the flavor improves over time, so they can be prepared well ahead of time, refrigerated, and simply reheated for company. This mole is best served with vegetables, tortillas, and rice.

POLLO CON MOLE AGRIDULCE

• CHICKEN BREAST WITH GUAJILLO SAUCE, SPICES, ORANGE, AND LIME •
• SERVES 4 •

5 guajillo chiles

1 cup water

2 cups plus 2 tablespoons canola oil

1½ white onions, coarsely chopped

3 cloves garlic

¼ fresh pineapple, peeled, cored, and cubed

¼ teaspoon ground canela

⅛ teaspoon ground allspice

⅛ teaspoon ground cloves

About 2 tablespoons kosher salt

½ cup freshly squeezed orange juice

1 tablespoon freshly squeezed lime juice

1½ cups chicken broth (page 201)

3 boneless, skinless whole chicken breasts, halved

Freshly ground black pepper

2 teaspoons unsalted butter

2 tablespoons sesame seeds, for garnish

....

CONTINUED

Place a dry skillet over medium heat. Add the chiles and toast for 2 to 3 minutes, pressing them into the pan and turning occasionally with tongs to prevent burning, until the skins lightly brown and the chiles begin to puff up. While the chiles are still hot, remove the stems but don't discard all the seeds since you'll want some for the heat. Submerge in a bowl of hot water for 20 to 30 minutes to rehydrate. Drain the chiles and combine with the water in a blender. Purée on high speed to make a paste.

Place a large skillet or sauté pan over high heat and add the 2 cups oil; you want a good depth so that the vegetables and pineapple will be submerged during frying. When the oil is hot, add the onion and fry for 3 to 4 minutes, until evenly browned around the edges and toward the center. Add the garlic cloves when the onion is about half-cooked and cook for 2 to 3 minutes, until browned. Remove the onion and garlic with a skimmer or slotted spoon and transfer to a colander or China cap to drain. Add a little more oil if necessary and carefully add the pineapple. Fry for 2 to 3 minutes, until golden brown. A spatter screen can be quite helpful since the juicy pineapple tends to spatter. Remove from the oil with a skimmer and add to the colander to drain. Wipe most of the oil out of the pan.

Place the onion, garlic, and pineapple in a blender and purée on high speed for 1 to 2 minutes, until a fine consistency is achieved. Return the purée to the pan and place over medium heat. Gently whisk in the chile purée, canela, allspice, and cloves, salt, orange juice, lime juice, and about ¾ cup of the broth. Decrease the heat to low and gently simmer for about 1 hour, until the flavors begin to marry. Adjust the seasoning with the spices and salt as necessary.

Preheat the oven to 350°F. Season both sides of the chicken with salt and pepper. Place a large sauté pan over high heat and add the 2 tablespoons oil and the butter. When hot, add the chicken and sauté for 5 to 7 minutes, until the first side is browned. Place the pan of chicken into the oven for about 10 minutes, until tender and cooked through. (The second side of the chicken will brown in the oven.)

Remove the chicken from the pan and arrange on individual plates or a serving platter. Place the pan back over high heat and add the remaining ¾ cup broth. Deglaze the pan, scraping up any browned bits with a wooden spoon, then simmer and reduce for 5 to 6 minutes. Add to the simmering sauce and ladle over the chicken. Serve at once, garnishing each plate with a sprinkling of sesame seeds.

The sauce in this dish can be applied to a number of different seafoods, including scallops, orange roughy, and red snapper. These white-fleshed fish are great foils for the unmistakably smooth and complex flavor of Agavero tequila liqueur. Serve this dish with rice and vegetables on the side.

PESCADO AL AGAVERO

• PETRALE SOLE WITH AGAVERO AND CAPERS •
• SERVES 4 •

1½ pounds petrale sole

Kosher salt

Freshly ground white pepper

3 tablespoons olive oil

1 teaspoon plus 6 tablespoons unsalted butter

2 tablespoons large capers packed in salt

1 serrano chile, finely chopped

½ cup Agavero tequila liqueur

½ cup shrimp broth (page 199)

Juice of 3 limes

½ bunch cilantro, stemmed and chopped

. . . .

Remove any residual bones or scales from the fish. Fold the ends of the fillets to the underside so the pieces are in almost rounded bundles. Season both sides of the fish with salt and pepper. Place a large sauté pan or skillet over high heat and add the oil. When the oil is hot, gently place the fish, flat side down, into the pan with the 1 teaspoon butter.

Gently shake the sauté pan a few times while adding the fillets to prevent sticking. Decrease the heat to medium and cook, turning once, for 4 to 7 minutes total cooking time, until an even brown crust has formed and the fish is firm to the touch. Add more oil and butter if necessary to help with the browning. Transfer the fish to a plate and keep warm.

Drain any excess oil from the pan. Add the capers and chile to the pan and sauté for 30 seconds. Remove the pan from the heat and add the Agavero to deglaze the pan, scraping up any browned bits with a wooden spoon. Return the pan to the stove top over high heat and cook for 1 minute, until the liquid is reduced by half. Add the broth and simmer for 3 to 4 minutes. Cut the 6 tablespoons butter into cubes. Whisk in the lime juice, cubed butter, and cilantro and heat gently for 30 to 60 seconds, until slightly thickened; do not boil. Adjust the seasoning with salt as necessary.

To serve, arrange the fish on individual plates and pour the sauce over. Serve at once.

This is a great dish for fall when sea scallops and hard squashes are both plentiful. A little bit of shrimp broth really helps to carry the heat from the chiles and the squash adds a nice contrasting sweetness and texture. Most of the entrées at the restaurant get either rice or tortillas, but you may want to serve both with this dish in order to sop up every last bit of sauce. Start searing the scallops while you are reducing the sauce, and both elements will come together quickly.

CALLOS CON CALABAZA

• SEARED SEA SCALLOPS WITH BUTTERNUT SQUASH, CHILES, AND ONIONS •
• SERVES 4 •

1½ pounds sea scallops

About 3 teaspoons kosher salt

Freshly ground black pepper

2 tablespoons canola oil

3 tablespoons unsalted butter

½ cup sliced shallots

2 cups finely diced butternut squash

¾ cup brandy

½ cup shrimp broth (page 199)

1 serrano chile, chopped

. . . .

Remove the hinge muscles from the scallops and pat them dry with a paper towel. Season both sides of the scallops with salt and pepper and set them aside while you start the sauce.

To make the sauce, heat a medium sauté pan over medium-high heat, and add 1 tablespoon each of the canola oil and the butter. Add the shallots and sauté for about 30 seconds, until translucent. Add the squash and cook for 5 to 7 minutes, until the edges begin to brown. Remove the pan from the

heat, add the brandy (it may flame up, so keep your face and hands away from the pan), and return to the heat to cook for 3 to 5 minutes, until the liquid is reduced by half. Stir in the broth and chile. Simmer 3 to 5 minutes, until the flavors marry and the squash is tender. Season the broth with salt and pepper and decrease the heat to low.

While the sauce is reducing, place a large sauté pan over high heat. When the pan is scalding hot, add the remaining tablespoon of oil and 1 more tablespoon of the butter. When the oil is hot, carefully add the scallops a few at time without splashing the oil. Decrease the heat to medium-high. Sear for 2 to 3 minutes, until nicely browned, then flip the scallops with tongs or a spatula. Sear the other side for 2 to 3 minutes, until browned. The whole cooking process should take 4 to 7 minutes.

Arrange the scallops on separate plates. Swirl the remaining 1 tablespoon butter into the sauce to thicken. Adjust the seasoning with salt as necessary and evenly spoon the sauce over the scallops. Serve at once.

For nicely done rare to medium-rare fish, have your fishmonger cut the tuna into even 6-ounce portions from a smaller part of the loin to assure 1-inch-thick steaks. The inspiration for this dish was a peppercorn crusted steak, after all. The coriander seeds are rather delicate but they help to offset the heat of the chile flakes. Besides packing some heat, the coriander and chile crust adds textural contrast to the tuna and really enhances its flavor.

ATÚN ENCOSTRADO DE CHILE Y CILANTRO

• CHILE DE ÁRBOL- AND CORIANDER-CRUSTED TUNA •
• SERVES 4 •

6 dried chiles de árbol
¼ cup whole coriander seeds
4 (¾- to 1-inch thick, 6-ounce) pieces
    sushi-grade ahi tuna
Kosher salt
Freshly ground black pepper
1 to 2 tablespoons canola oil
4 tablespoons unsalted butter, cubed
2 shallots, chopped
1 serrano chile, stemmed and chopped
¾ cup Agavero tequila liqueur
⅓ bunch cilantro, stemmed and chopped

. . . .

Place a dry skillet over medium heat. Add the chiles de árbol and toast for 2 to 3 minutes, pressing them into the pan and turning occasionally with tongs to prevent burning, until puffed up and slightly browned. Remove the stems and allow to cool at room temperature. Chop the chile meat, skins, and seeds into flakes and place in a small bowl. Place the coriander seeds on a cutting board and lightly crack them with the back of a pan. Add to the chile flakes.

Sprinkle both sides of the tuna with salt and pepper. Dip the fish into the chile-coriander mixture to form a crust on all sides. Place a large sauté pan over high heat and add the oil. When the oil is hot, place the fish into the pan and add 1 tablespoon of the butter to help with the browning process. Decrease the heat to medium-high and cook for 4 to 7 minutes, until browned on all sides. The center should still be raw; be careful not to burn the crust.

Transfer the tuna to a plate. Return the pan to the stove top over medium heat and add the shallots. Sauté for about 30 seconds. Add the serrano chile and sauté for 30 seconds. Remove the pan from the heat and add the Agavero. Return the pan to high heat and simmer for 3 to 6 minutes, until reduced by two-thirds. Turn the heat off then gradually whisk in the remaining 3 tablespoons butter to give the sauce a little more body. Add the cilantro and taste and adjust the seasoning with salt as necessary.

To serve, arrange the fish on individual plates and pour the sauce over. Serve immediately.

While sesame seeds are often associated with Asian and Indian dishes, they are actually quite common in Mexican cuisine, frequently used in moles and other sauces. In this preparation, the sweet, nutty creaminess of the sesame seeds is a wonderful accompaniment to the toasty bitterness of the pumpkin seeds and the heat from the chile purée. We often enjoy this dish during the late summer at Doña Tomás and serve it with corn pudding (page 138) and puréed black beans (page 134).

Preferably, your tuna will be from the center of the loin since the tail pieces are often quite sinewy. To get the red onion perfectly thin, we rely on Juan's culinary precision at Doña Tomás. If your knife skills aren't quite up to snuff, use a mandoline.

ATÚN DEL DIABLO

• SEARED ALBACORE TUNA WITH PUMPKIN SEED-SESAME SAUCE
AND PICKLED RED ONIONS •

• SERVES 6 •

PICKLED ONIONS

Olive oil

1 clove garlic, thinly sliced

¼ cup apple cider vinegar

1 scant teaspoon kosher salt

1 pinch dried oregano

1 pinch dried cumin

1 pinch ground allspice

1 red onion, sliced paper thin and
    submerged in cold water for 1 hour

PUMPKIN SEED-SESAME SAUCE

4 dried chiles de árbol

2 teaspoons canola oil

¼ cup pepitas, hulled

¼ cup sesame seeds

3 teaspoons apple cider vinegar

½ cup warm water

1 clove garlic

Kosher salt

6 (1- to 1½-inch-thick, 6-ounce)
    albacore tuna steaks

Kosher salt

Freshly ground white pepper

3 tablespoons canola oil

2 teaspoons unsalted butter, at
    room temperature

¼ bunch cilantro, stemmed and
    chopped, for garnish

. . . .

CONTINUED

To prepare the onions, place a small sauté pan over medium-high heat and add a splash of oil. Sauté the garlic for 30 seconds, until lightly perfumed and translucent. Transfer the garlic to a small bowl and add the vinegar, salt, oregano, cumin, and allspice. Mix well. Gently squeeze the water from the onions and add them to the bowl. Toss well to coat. Allow the onions to marinate at room temperature for at least 1 hour but no more than 2 hours before serving.

To prepare the sauce, place a dry skillet over medium heat. Add the chiles and toast for about 2 minutes, pressing them into the pan and turning occasionally with tongs to prevent burning, until they turn light brown and give off a sharp aroma. While the chiles are still hot, remove the stems and submerge in a bowl of hot water for about 10 minutes to rehydrate. Drain and transfer the chiles to a blender.

Place a sauté pan over high heat and add the oil. When the oil is hot, add the pumpkin seeds, decrease the heat to medium-high, and toss the seeds for 2 to 3 minutes, until they begin to brown and become evenly crisp. Transfer the pumpkin seeds to the blender. Place the sesame seeds in the pan over medium heat. Toast for 5 to 7 minutes, until browned. Transfer to the blender.

Add the vinegar and water to the blender and process on high speed for about 1 minute, until puréed. Add the garlic and salt to taste and continue to blend for 1 minute, until the sauce is the consistency of a wet cake batter. Adjust the seasoning with salt and the consistency with water as necessary. Use immediately or cover and refrigerate for up to 1 week.

Season the tuna on both sides with salt and pepper. Place a large sauté pan over high heat and add the oil. When the oil is smoking, add the tuna, shaking the pan to prevent sticking. Decrease the heat to medium-high and cook for 3 to 4 minutes, until crisp and brown on the first side. Add the butter and flip the tuna. Cook for another 3 to 4 minutes, until the second side is crisp and brown.

To serve, arrange the tuna steaks on a platter or individual plates and spoon the warm sauce over each. Garnish each with a large three-finger pinch of the pickled onions and a pinch of the cilantro. Serve at once.

The inspiration for this dish came from a recent visit to the open-air markets in Oaxaca, where large vats of mustard powder were to be found among the bags of vibrant red chile powders, sacks of avocados, and stacks of *hoja santa* leaves. Here we're using Dijon mustard instead of mustard powder, which gives the sauce more richness and less heat. The sauce is appropriately balanced with the sweetness of the mead and the smokiness of the *chile de árbol* powder. If you have trouble finding agave mead, substitute a mixture of tequila and mead, or tequila mixed with a teaspoon of honey and a splash of white wine.

PESCADO CON SALSA MOSTAZA

• ATLANTIC COD WITH MUSTARD SAUCE •

• SERVES 4 •

4 (6-ounce) Atlantic cod fillets

Kosher salt

Freshly ground black pepper

1 tablespoon canola oil

2½ teaspoons unsalted butter

2 shallots, sliced

¼ cup agave mead

¼ cup chicken broth (page 201)

1 cup heavy whipping cream

¾ teaspoon powdered chile de árbol

1½ teaspoons Dijon mustard

. . . .

Preheat the oven to 350°F. Season both sides of the fish with salt and pepper. Place a large sauté pan over high heat and add the oil. When the oil is hot, gently add the fish, top side down, shaking the pan to prevent sticking. Decrease the heat to medium-high and add 1 teaspoon of the butter. Cook for 4 to 5 minutes, until the edges begin to brown. Carefully flip the fillets with a spatula and cook for 3 to 4 minutes, until lightly browned on the other side. Transfer the fillets to a baking sheet.

Add the remaining 1½ teaspoons butter and the shallots to the pan over high heat. Sauté for 30 seconds, until translucent. Add the mead and broth and cook for 5 to 10 minutes, until reduced by half. Add the cream, bring to a boil, then decrease the heat to medium. Simmer for 5 to 7 minutes, until the sauce begins to thicken. Place the fish in the oven for 3 to 4 minutes, until firm to the touch. To test doneness, gently slit open one of the fillets; the flesh should still be moist and just opaque.

Whisk the chile powder and mustard into the sauce and adjust the seasoning with salt as necessary. Remove the fish from the oven and arrange on plates. Ladle the sauce over each piece and serve at once.

This dish represents a clash of two borders with its Alaskan-caught halibut and Latino-inspired dried oregano and *hoja santa*. Because Pacific halibut gets so large, the cheek itself is actually big enough to be edible. The texture of the cheeks is more firm than the rest of the fish, similar to a scallop in mouthfeel, with the familiar mild halibut flavor. If you can't find halibut cheeks, try substituting scallops, halibut fillets, or any other dense, white-fleshed fish with this recipe.

PESCADO A LA VERACRUZANA

• SAUTÉED HALIBUT CHEEKS WITH TOMATOES, CAPERS, AND OLIVES •
• SERVES 4 •

5 ripe Early Girl tomatoes

¼ cup canola oil

½ onion, cut into ¼-inch dice

1 teaspoon chopped garlic

1 teaspoon chopped serrano chile

¼ cup sliced green olives

1½ tablespoons capers

About 1 teaspoon kosher salt

1 pinch powdered hoja santa

1 pinch dried oregano

24 ounces halibut cheeks

Freshly ground black pepper

2 teaspoons unsalted butter

. . . .

Preheat the oven to 350°F. Place the tomatoes in a baking dish and roast, turning as necessary, for 30 to 40 minutes, until the skins blacken evenly. Transfer the tomatoes and their juices to a food processor and pulse to roughly chop.

Place a large sauté pan over high heat and add 2 tablespoons of the oil. Add the onion and sauté for 3 to 5 minutes, until translucent. Add the garlic and chile and cook, stirring, for 15 seconds. Add the tomatoes, olives, and capers. Decrease the heat to medium and simmer for 3 to 4 minutes, until the flavors marry. Remove from the heat. Carefully adjust the seasoning with salt (the capers and olives will have a lot). Stir in the *hoja santa* and oregano.

In a separate sauté pan, heat the remaining 2 tablespoons oil over high heat. Season both sides of the fish with salt and pepper. When the oil is hot, add the butter to help brown the fish. Add the fish and decrease the heat to medium-high. Sauté, turning once, for 4 to 7 minutes, until both sides are evenly browned and the center is medium-rare to medium.

Arrange the fish on plates or a platter, cover with the sauce, and serve at once.

Surprisingly, we've found that this dish works better with canned pumpkin than with fresh. The fresh pumpkin tends to be wetter and starchier after cooking and doesn't create as even and smooth a purée as the canned pumpkin does. Experiment with various brands to find a quality pumpkin with the least tinny flavor.

CREMA DE CALABAZA

• PUMPKIN CREAM •
• SERVES 6 •

2 tablespoons cold water

2 teaspoons powdered gelatin

1 cup heavy whipping cream

½ cup granulated sugar

1¼ cups sour cream

¾ cup canned pumpkin purée

⅓ cup mascarpone cheese

1 teaspoon pure vanilla extract

¼ teaspoon Grand Marnier

¼ teaspoon ground canela

1 cup lightly sweetened whipped cream

Place the cold water in a small bowl and sprinkle the gelatin powder over. Allow to sit for 3 to 5 minutes, until all the water has been absorbed.

Bring a pot of water to a boil. In a large stainless steel bowl, whisk together the whipping cream, sugar, sour cream, pumpkin purée, and mascarpone. Place the bowl over the boiling water and heat gradually for 5 to 10 minutes, until the sugar melts, whisking occasionally to prevent curdling. Add the gelatin and whisk for another 5 to 10 minutes, until the mixture reaches 150°F and the gelatin is evenly melted and dispersed. Whisk in the vanilla, Grand Marnier, and canela. Taste and adjust the spice and liquor seasoning as necessary.

Strain the mixture through a China cap into a fresh bowl. Evenly divide the custard among six 8-ounce ramekins or glass bowls. Cover and refrigerate for at least 4 hours, until the custard becomes firm and puddinglike. To serve, top each custard with a dollop of the whipped cream and enjoy at once. Individually wrap any of the custards not being served and store refrigerated for up to 3 days.

Pineapples are said to have originated in the lush lowlands of Paraguay, making their way into Mexico long before Captain Cook sailed them over to Hawaii in the late 1700s. The ripeness of a pineapple is not judged by its color, but by its smell, feel, and appearance. The crown should be green and fresh and the body firm without any soft spots or bruises. Once pineapples have been picked they will not get any sweeter (though they can get less acidic), so use them as soon as possible after purchase. If necessary, pineapples may be refrigerated for a few weeks to prolong shelf life.

This hot dessert blends the spice of rum with the sweetness of pineapple and contrasts its dense, firm texture with a light crunchy layer of puff pastry. Puff pastry can be found in the freezer section of most grocery stores, or you can make your own. The sauce, pineapple, and crema can all be made ahead of time, but the pastry shouldn't be baked until just before serving. Defrost the puff pastry 20 to 30 minutes before you're ready to start rolling and cutting (you want it as cold as possible while you're working with it).

POSTRE DE PIÑA

• PUFF PASTRY WITH ROASTED PINEAPPLE, CREMA, AND
RUM-BUTTER SAUCE •

• SERVES 6 •

RUM SAUCE

1/3 cup heavy whipping cream

6 tablespoons cold unsalted butter, diced

2 teaspoons pure vanilla extract

3/4 cup granulated sugar

2 to 3 tablespoons water

3 tablespoons Myers's dark rum

1 pinch kosher salt

6 (1-inch-thick) round slices fresh pineapple, cored

3 tablespoons granulated sugar

1/3 cup fresh pineapple juice

1 (9 by 18-inch) sheet puff pastry

1 egg yolk

2 tablespoons whole milk

1/2 cup crema, for garnish (page 198)

CONTINUED

To prepare the sauce, combine the cream, butter, and vanilla in a small saucepan over medium-high heat. Bring to a gentle boil, being careful to not scorch the bottom. Place a separate sauté pan over medium-high heat. Pile the granulated sugar in the center of the pan and drizzle the edges of the pile with the water to prevent burning. As the sugar begins to heat, fold the melted edges into the center, gently stirring to break up any large lumps and prevent the syrup from sticking and burning on the sides. Melt the sugar for 7 to 10 minutes, until it thins and turns an even shade of reddish brown.

Increase the heat to high, carefully add about 1 tablespoon of the rum, and allow the mixture to flambé. Once the flames die down, carefully whisk in one-third of the cream-butter mixture. Alternate this process 2 more times until all the rum and cream have been added. This method will prevent the sauce from becoming too thick (and breaking) or too thin (and not emulsifying). Bring the sauce to a full boil and add a pinch of salt to bring out the flavors. Set aside.

Preheat the oven to 350°F. Line a baking sheet with aluminum foil. Sprinkle both sides of the pineapple slices liberally with the sugar and place on the prepared baking sheet. Bake for 20 minutes, then drizzle the slices with the pineapple juice. Meanwhile, take the puff pastry out of the freezer to defrost. Continue to baste with the juice for 10 to 20 minutes, until the pineapple is fork-tender.

When the puff pastry is defrosted but still cold, roll it out on a well-floured surface, stretching slightly both lengthwise and widthwise. Select a bowl with a 4-inch diameter to use as a template. Place the bowl upside down on the pastry, and cut around the edge with a sharp knife. You should get 6 rounds of pastry. Place the dough rounds on a baking sheet lined with wax paper or a silicone baking mat; prick each dough round with a fork. Whisk the egg yolk and milk together in a small bowl. Evenly brush the egg wash on the dough rounds. Bake for 15 to 20 minutes, until the pastry rises and is golden brown.

Place 1 piece of the puff pastry on each plate. Place a slice of warm pineapple on each and cover with the sauce. Drizzle with crema right before serving.

Much of the soul and folklore of Mexican cuisine stems from the three pre-Columbian staples of the Americas: corn, beans, and squash. Corn and beans manage to make an appearance in just about every dish at Doña Tomás and Tacubaya, so we are always searching for creative ways to balance the "three sisters" by incorporating more members of the squash family. According to tradition, these three crops are to be planted, cooked, and consumed together, and who are we to disregard history?

Though we often sauté zucchini as an accompaniment for dinner entrées, its natural sweetness and tender texture also make it a perfect candidate for dessert. While this cake is not a traditional Mexican dish by any means, the canela adds enough character for the zucchini to sit in good company with her sisters in this book.

PASTEL DE CALABACITA

• ZUCCHINI CAKE •
• SERVES 8 •

3 eggs
2 cups granulated sugar
1 cup canola oil
2 teaspoons pure vanilla extract
2 cups grated zucchini (about 2 medium zucchinis)
3 cups all-purpose flour
1 teaspoon baking soda
¼ teaspoon baking powder
1 teaspoon kosher salt
Confectioners' sugar
1 tablespoon ground canela

. . . .

Preheat the oven to 350°F. Coat the sides and bottom of a 10-inch round cake pan with butter.

Beat the eggs with a whisk in a large bowl. Add the granulated sugar, canola oil, and vanilla and mix well. Stir in the zucchini. In a separate bowl, sift together the flour, baking soda, baking powder, and salt. Add the dry ingredients to the wet ingredients, gently folding them in with a spatula until a thick, smooth batter is achieved. Pour the batter into the prepared pan and bake for about 1 hour, until golden brown and firm yet somewhat spongy. A toothpick or small knife inserted in the center should come out clean.

Allow the cake to cool for 5 to 10 minutes in the pan before turning it out onto a cooling rack. Allow to cool completely. To serve, cut the cake into pieces, place on dessert plates, and dust with the confectioners' sugar and canela.

The crema gives this cake a truly dense, decadent character. Just about any fruit can be used—blackberries and fresh nectarines are great in the summer, and pineapple is a favorite during the off-season. If using a liquidy fruit like pineapple, be sure to cook it down so it doesn't extrude too much juice. Creating an even, thin layer of fruit and allowing the cake to thoroughly cool are important factors to a successful cake. Too much fruit and the cake will taste great, but the batter in the center won't cook through. And if you cut into it before it's cool, you'll end up with an oozy, formless slice on your plate. The cake is best when accompanied by whipped cream or ice cream.

PASTEL DE CANELA CON MORAS

• CINNAMON-CRÈME FRAÎCHE CAKE WITH BLACKBERRIES •
• SERVES 6 TO 8 •

1½ cups chopped pecans

½ cup plus 1 tablespoon packed dark brown sugar

4 to 6 tablespoons plus 2 cups granulated sugar

2½ teaspoons ground canela

2 nectarines, halved, pitted, and cut into
⅛-inch slices

2 pints blackberries

1 cup cold unsalted butter, diced

1 tablespoon grated lemon zest

1 tablespoon baking powder

½ teaspoon salt

2 eggs

2 cups crema (page 198)

1 tablespoon pure vanilla extract

3 cups all-purpose flour, sifted

Preheat the oven to 325°F. Spread the pecans on a baking sheet and toast, stirring occasionally, for 3 to 5 minutes, until evenly browned. Watch the nuts carefully while they're in the oven since they can burn quickly. Remove from the oven and allow to cool. Increase the oven temperature to 350°F.

In a small bowl, combine the pecans, brown sugar, and canela and mix well. In a separate bowl, combine 4 to 6 tablespoons of the granulated sugar (more or less depending on the tartness of the fruit), the nectarines, and the blackberries and gently toss to coat.

Combine the butter, lemon zest, baking powder, salt, and 2 cups sugar in a stand mixer fitted with the paddle attachment. Mix on medium-high speed until creamy and light in color. In a separate bowl, whisk together the eggs, crema, and vanilla. Add to the mixer and beat on medium speed until a wet, runny batter is formed. Slowly add the flour in three parts, mixing on low speed and scraping down the bottom and sides, until a stiff dough forms.

Lightly butter or spray the bottom and sides of a 10-inch springform pan. Pour half of the batter into the pan. Evenly sprinkle one-third of the pecan mixture over the batter. Evenly spread the fruit mixture over the nuts. Pour the rest of the batter into the pan and sprinkle the top of the cake with the remaining two-thirds of the pecan mixture.

Bake for 1 hour to 1 hour, 15 minutes, until the center of the cake can be pierced with a wooden skewer and come out clean. The finished cake should be browned and have a firm but spongy feel. Allow the cake to cool in the pan for about 30 minutes. Gently loosen the edges of the cake by running a butter knife around the perimeter of the pan. Remove the sides of the pan. Flip the cake out onto a plate and remove the bottom of the pan. Gently flip the cake right side up onto a baking sheet and let it cool for at least 2 hours before cutting.

This traditional Mexican dessert is soaked in three different milks to achieve a divine richness, hence the name *tres leches*, "three milks." You often see evaporated milk, sweetened condensed milk, and heavy cream used for this preparation, but we like to do things a little different at Doña Tomás. Instead of evaporated milk we use *cajeta*, a creamy caramel that can be made with full-fat goat's or cow's milk. It gives the cake a little more body.

PASTEL DE TRES LECHES

• "THREE MILKS" CAKE WITH FRESH STRAWBERRIES •
• SERVES 10 TO 12 •

6 eggs
1 cup plus 2 tablespoons granulated sugar
6 tablespoons unsalted butter, melted
1 cup all-purpose flour, sifted
1½ pints strawberries, sliced
²/₃ cup cajeta, at room temperature (page 62)
²/₃ cup sweetened condensed milk
1½ cups plus 1 quart heavy whipping cream
1 tablespoon pure vanilla extract
1 cup confectioners' sugar, sifted

. . . .

Preheat the oven to 350°F and center the baking rack. Line a 10-inch cake pan with a piece of parchment or wax paper and lightly grease the paper and sides of the pan with nonstick spray or butter.

Bring a pot of water to a boil. Combine the eggs and 1 cup granulated sugar in a stainless steel bowl and whisk together. Place the bowl over the boiling water and whisk constantly for about 10 minutes, until the mixture doubles in volume, turns pale and fluffy, and forms ribbonlike folds off the end of the whisk.

CONTINUED

Gently fold in the butter and flour. Pour the batter into the prepared cake pan (it should be about 1 inch deep). Bake for about 40 minutes, until doubled in height, golden brown, fluffy, and cooked through (an inserted wooden skewer should come out clean). Turn the cake out onto a cooling rack and allow to cool completely. Remove the paper.

Set 4 to 5 evenly shaped strawberries aside for garnish. In a bowl, toss the remaining strawberries with the 2 tablespoons granulated sugar. In a separate bowl, combine the *cajeta,* condensed milk, and 1½ cups whipping cream and mix well. In a separate bowl, using an electric mixer on high speed, whip the 1 quart whipping cream to medium peaks. Add the vanilla and confectioners' sugar toward the end of the whipping process.

Slice the cake in half crosswise using a long serrated knife. Place the bottom half of the cake on a serving plate. On a separate plate, place the top half of the cake with the cut side up. Using a tablespoon, spoon half of the three-milk mixture over the bottom of the cake, so it is soaked evenly. The milk should absorb right into the cake. Using half of the remaining three-milk mixture, soak the top of the cake.

Spread a ⅛-inch layer of the whipped cream evenly over the bottom half of the cake. Arrange a thin layer of the strawberries on top. Cover with another thin layer of whipped cream and another thin layer of strawberries. Finish with one more thin layer of cream. Place the top half of the cake on top of the cream and strawberry layers, cut side down.

Soak the very top of the cake with the remaining three-milk mixture. Cover the entire cake with the remaining whipped cream, spreading evenly over the top and sides. Decorate the top of the cake with the reserved strawberry slices. Refrigerate for at least 2 hours before slicing and serving. Any leftovers must be stored in the refrigerator.

This dessert has a decadent sweetness that satisfies palates from Mexico all the way back to its Latin origins in Spain. Flan was introduced to Europeans by the Romans, although many of their applications were savory dishes such as fish or eel, which probably didn't fair so well with many a sweet tooth.

The rose water gives the custard a nice floral flavor and can be purchased in the baking and pastry aisle of most specialty stores. Or, if you have fresh roses free of pesticides and fungicides, you can make your own: Boil 1 cup petals with 1 cup water and 1 tablespoon honey for about 10 minutes, until the color leeches out of the petals. Steep overnight at room temperature and then pass through a fine-mesh strainer. The water can be covered and refrigerated for up to 2 weeks.

FLAN DE ROSAS

• ROSE PETAL FLAN •
• SERVES 6 •

TOPPING
¾ cup granulated sugar
2 to 3 tablespoons water

CUSTARD
4 cups whole milk
1 cup granulated sugar
4 eggs
4 egg yolks
⅓ teaspoon pure vanilla extract
2 teaspoons rose water

To prepare the topping, place a sauté pan over medium-high heat. Pile the granulated sugar in the center of the pan and drizzle the edges of the pile with the water to prevent burning. As the sugar begins to heat, fold the melted edges into the center, gently stirring to break up any large lumps and prevent the syrup from sticking and burning on the sides. Melt the sugar for 7 to 10 minutes, until it thins and turns an even shade of reddish brown.

CONTINUED

Quickly divide the sugar among six 8-ounce ramekins, swirling each ramekin so that an even layer forms. The sugar will make a crackling noise as it cools but rest assured—it is the sugar and not your ramekins. Place the ramekins into a 2-inch-deep baking dish.

Preheat the oven to 350°F and center the rack. To prepare the custard, combine the milk and sugar in a small saucepan over medium-high heat. Cook for 7 to 10 minutes, until the sugar is melted and the mixture reaches 120°F; do not let the milk boil. In a bowl, whisk together the eggs, egg yolks, vanilla, and rose water. When the milk is warm, place a couple ladlefuls into the egg mixture, whisking constantly so the eggs do not cook. After a few ladles of milk have been added, quickly add the egg mixture back into the pot of milk. Decrease the heat to low and whisk for 30 seconds, until warm and incorporated.

Ladle the custard into the ramekins, filling to about ¼ inch from the rim. Place the pan of ramekins in the oven and fill it halfway with warm water. Bake for 1 hour, until the custard is congealed but ideally not browned. If you shake a ramekin, the custard should jiggle somewhat like Jell-O.

Carefully remove the ramekins from the pan and cool in the refrigerator for 2 hours. To serve, gently separate the flan from the sides of the ramekins with a sharp knife and turn out onto dessert plates. The caramelized sugar will have liquefied in the bottom of the ramekin to form a sauce. Any leftovers can be covered and refrigerated for 2 to 3 days.

This is a great summer dessert, reminiscent of Key lime pie—though I've never used a Key lime in my life. Bitter oranges, Key limes, and Persian limes are all available in the tropical climate of Mexico, and all will work here—I use Persian limes for this pie, and it tastes great. We do not, however, recommend using the little green plastic bottles of lime juice with the yellow tops. Freshly whipped cream makes a great topping for this dessert.

PAY DE LIMA

• LIME PIE •

• SERVES 6 •

GRAHAM CRACKER CRUST

1⅓ cups graham cracker crumbs
    (about 1 sleeve of crackers)
1 tablespoon granulated sugar
5 tablespoons unsalted butter, melted

FILLING

4 eggs
1½ cups granulated sugar
1 teaspoon grated lime zest
¾ cup freshly squeezed lime juice
    (from 8 to 9 limes)
½ cup unsalted butter, at room
    temperature, diced

To prepare the crust, combine the cracker crumbs, sugar, and butter in a bowl and mix until they come together. Using your fingers, press the crumbs evenly into the bottom and sides of a 9-inch pie pan. The crust should be about ¼ inch thick all the way around.

To prepare the filling, bring a pot of water to a boil. Combine the eggs, sugar, lime zest, and lime juice in a stainless steel bowl. Place the bowl over the boiling water and whisk constantly for 15 minutes, until the mixture doubles in size, turns frothy and opaque, and forms ribbonlike folds off the end of the whisk. Gradually add the butter and whisk until completely melted.

Pour the batter into the crust and refrigerate for at least 6 hours before slicing and serving. Any leftovers can be covered and refrigerated for up to 3 days.

The mojito (right) may be king, but the Reina is definitely the queen of all drinks. A true margarita should be enjoyed chilled, but definitely not blended. We use a high-quality silver tequila for a cleaner, more refined flavor. The essence of the blue agave should remain unadulterated by the heavy oak flavor characteristic of a reposado or añejo tequila. Too much simple syrup or too much lime will also upset the balance of the sweet and sour tones. When made right, all the flavors should gently strike the palate in harmony.

LEFT TO RIGHT: DAIQUIRI DE PEPINO (PAGE 194); TOMÁS COLLINS (PAGE 194); MOJITO (THIS PAGE); SANGRÍA SANDÍA (PAGE 119); DOÑA COLADA (PAGE 195).

We put this drink on the menu when we first opened and originally used rum. Eventually we decided that the mint came through much cleaner when using *cachaça* (pronounced kah-sha-sah), a distilled sugarcane spirit. We prefer Pirassununga 51, but any brand of *cachaça* can be used.

MARGARITA LA REINA
• QUEEN MARGARITA •
• SERVES 1 •

Coarse salt
4 tablespoons simple syrup (page 204)
Juice of 1½ to 2 limes
5 counts silver tequila, preferably El Tesoro
2 counts Cointreau liqueur
1 lime wedge

. . . .

Salt the rim of a chilled margarita glass. In a pint glass filled with cubed ice, combine the syrup, lime juice, tequila, and Cointreau. Cover with a bar shaker and shake vigorously for 5 seconds. Strain into the prepared glass. Garnish with the lime wedge and enjoy.

MOJITO
• MUDDLED CACHAÇA AND MINT COCKTAIL •
• SERVES 1 •

5 to 6 large mint leaves
4 teaspoons simple syrup (page 204)
5 counts cachaça or rum
Juice of 1 lime
2 counts club soda
1 lime wedge

. . . .

Fill a pint glass with cubed ice. Add the mint leaves and syrup. With a muddler (see page 32) or the back of a bar spoon, smash the ingredients in the bottom of the glass for 1 to 2 minutes, until a slushlike consistency is achieved. Scrape down the sides of the glass to make sure you incorporate all the mint. The ice should be slushy or frothy and the mint should be broken into tiny flecks.

Add the *cachaça* and lime juice, cover with a bar shaker, and shake vigorously. Pour the entire contents into a clean pint glass. Top off with the club soda, garnish with the lime wedge, and serve with straws wide enough to pick up the flecks of mint.

This drink was created after one of our regular patrons brought us back a small bag of worm salt from Oaxaca. Worm salt (which actually has ground-up grubs in it) usually comes with bottles of mezcal, but our former bartender, Paul, came up with a non-mezcal use for the salt—this refreshing cucumber daiquiri. This version uses coarse salt mixed with chile rather than worm salt.

Families in England, Australia, and America all lay claim to the traditional Tom Collins, but only Doña Tomás is known for its Tomás Collins. Our Collins is very similar to the original, although our substitution of Cointreau and lime juice for superfine sugar and lemon juice gives it a distinctive flair. We feel it's important to adopt traditional drinks to match what we're doing with our food. Drinks such as this fit in well with our use of traditional Mexican flavors and local California ingredients.

DAIQUIRI DE PEPINO

• CUCUMBER DAIQUIRI •
• SERVES 1 •

TOMÁS COLLINS

• TOM COLLINS •
• SERVES 1 •

5 counts rum, preferably Flor de Caña
4 teaspoons simple syrup (page 204)
Juice of 1½ limes
1½ inches cucumber, sliced
Coarse salt
Chile powder
1 cucumber wedge

Coarse sugar
Juice of 1½ limes
4 teaspoons simple syrup (page 204)
2 counts Cointreau liqueur
5 counts gin, preferably Tanqueray Ten
2 counts club soda, preferably Canada Dry
1 lime wheel

....

....

Pour the rum and syrup into a pint glass filled with cubed iced. Add the lime juice and sliced cucumber. With a muddler (see page 32) or the back of a bar spoon, smash the ingredients in the bottom of the glass for 1 to 2 minutes, until slushy and frothy. Salt the rim of a tall glass with coarse salt and chile powder. Strain the daiquiri into the glass and garnish with the cucumber wedge. Drink at once.

Sugar the rim of a tall glass and fill with cubed ice. Fill a pint glass with cubed ice and add the lime juice, syrup, Cointreau, and gin. Cover with a bar shaker and shake until blended. Strain into the prepared glass. Top off with the club soda, garnish with the lime wheel, and enjoy.

There is no way we could have a Tomás Collins without a Doña Colada. Like many Piña Colada recipes, ours calls for cream of coconut, a blend of coconut cream (the meat and milk) with natural cane sugar. Unlike the original 1954 Piña Colada recipe, we omit the piña, or pineapple, and use simple syrup and lime juice. The taste is still creamy and sweet, a little more acidic but just as tropical.

It's said that in the early 1900s, this original concoction of brandy, Triple Sec, and lime juice was often served to a patron who would arrive at Harry's Bar in Paris via the sidecar of a motorcycle. Like others, we use Cointreau instead of Triple Sec, although we also add a touch of simple syrup to give it more sweetness. We have appropriately named the drink for a new generation of mechanical oddities—hydraulic shocks not included.

DOÑA COLADA

- LIME COLADA -
- SERVES 1 -

5 count Myers's light rum
4 teaspoons simple syrup (page 204)
Juice of 1 lime
1½ ounces cream of coconut, preferably Coco López
1 lime wedge

. . . .

Fill a pint glass with ice and pour the ice in a blender. Add the rum, syrup, lime juice, and cream of coconut and blend on high speed for about 1 minute, until completely crushed and slushy. If the drink is too thick and doesn't spin in the blender, add a few more cubes of ice. Pour into a wide, stemmed glass, garnish with the lime wedge, and enjoy.

LOWRIDER

- SIDECAR -
- SERVES 1 -

Coarse sugar
5 counts brandy
4 teaspoons simple syrup (page 204)
2 counts Cointreau liqueur
Juice of 1 lime
1 lime wedge

. . . .

Sugar the rim of a chilled martini glass. In a shaker with some cubed ice, combine the brandy, syrup, Cointreau, and lime juice. Cover with a bar shaker and shake well. Strain into the prepared glass, garnish with the lime wedge, and serve.

This chapter provides recipes for the important stocks, sauces, and accompaniments used in this book. At our restaurants, we keep large quantities of all of these items on hand, so that they are always available at a moment's notice. Obviously most home cooks won't have a gallon of chicken stock just waiting to be used, or ever have use for a whole quart of chile purée. We have therefore adjusted all these recipes to make smaller batches and tried to match the serving size of specific dishes. We want to make it as simple as possible for you to prepare and use these items at home, since your dishes will come out much more delicious with homemade stocks, for example, than store-bought ones.

CALDOS Y LADOS

BROTHS AND SAUCES

Crema accompanies a number of our dishes at Doña Tomás and Tacubaya, usually as a drizzled garnish over such items as rellenos. Its soft, rich body helps to counterbalance the spiciness of many of our sauces. Its mild, sour flavor also makes it a welcome addition to some desserts, most notably our crème fraîche cake (page 182), with its tart blackberries and spicy cinnamon.

Crema can be purchased in the dairy section of most supermarkets, either as "Mexican crema" or as the French crème fraîche. Sour cream is a cheaper alternative, although not as tasty. This recipe will yield a healthy 2-cup batch. Although none of the recipes call for that much, you'll probably want to have some in your fridge for a variety of applications.

CREMA

• CRÈME FRAÎCHE •
• MAKES 2⅓ CUPS •

2 cups heavy whipping cream
6 tablespoons buttermilk

. . . .

Place the cream and buttermilk in a large plastic or stainless steel container and mix well with a wire whisk. (Do not use an aluminum container; the metal will react with the cream, yielding a gray, metallic product.) Cover and allow the mixture to sit at room temperature for about 3 days. The resulting crema will be off-white and thick with a very mellow sour taste, not quite as thick or pungent as sour cream. The crema can be covered and refrigerated for up to 3 weeks.

Broth, *caldo,* made from shrimp shells essentially follows the same preparation as any other broth made with bones and meat. Raw shrimp shells are the key ingredient. Whenever we use shrimp at the restaurant, we will wrap and freeze the shells until we have enough to make a few gallons of stock. Two pounds of shrimp will yield the ½ pound of shells you need for this recipe. The shells can be frozen for months at a time, but keep in mind that they tend to sauté more evenly and give off more flavor when defrosted the night before cooking. You'll need a good fine-mesh strainer or chinois to press the shells through in order to extract the maximum shrimp essence. Shrimp bases are available in most specialty stores and can be substituted, but they aren't nearly as rich and don't yield the same clarity or unadulterated finish as a good homemade stock.

CALDO DE CAMARÓN

• SHRIMP BROTH •
• MAKES 1 QUART •

3 tablespoons olive oil
½ pound shrimp shells
1 white onion, chopped
2 celery stalks, chopped
1 large carrot, chopped
3 bay leaves
10 peppercorns
Kosher salt
About 1 quart cold water

Heat a large pot over high heat and add the oil. When the oil reaches its smoking point, add the shrimp shells and cook, stirring occasionally, for 30 seconds or so, until vibrant reddish orange. Add the onion, celery, and carrot, decrease the heat to medium, and sauté for 2 to 3 minutes, until soft and translucent. Add the bay leaves and peppercorns and a few pinches of salt.

Add the water and bring to a boil. Decrease the heat to achieve a gentle simmer and cook for 30 to 40 minutes. Adjust the seasoning with salt as necessary. Pass the stock through a fine-mesh strainer, pressing the shells and vegetables with the back of a ladle to extract all of the flavorful juice. Discard the solids.

Use at once or allow to cool, then cover and refrigerate for 2 to 3 days or freeze for up to 3 months.

Traditionally, stock is made with only bones, while broth is made from both the bones of the animal and the meat. The bones add natural gelatin to the broth, which is what makes it become firm when refrigerated, and the meat gives rich flavor.

Always start your broths or stocks with cold water and allow them to simmer slowly and reduce, as opposed to rapidly boiling them. The meat will end up more evenly cooked and you'll steep more flavor out of the bones. It is good practice to skim off the fat and impurities with a ladle throughout the cooking process; the care you take will come through in the flavor of the final product. All soup recipes made with *caldo de pollo* are set for one broth recipe, which serves 6 people. However, only about ¼ of the meat, or 2 cups, will be needed for those soups; the rest can be used in other dishes.

CALDO DE POLLO

• CHICKEN BROTH AND SHREDDED CHICKEN •

• MAKES 1½ QUARTS BROTH AND ABOUT 2 POUNDS SHREDDED CHICKEN MEAT •

1 (4-pound) fryer or roasting chicken
½ white onion, diced
1 celery stalk, chopped
1 small carrot, chopped
2 bay leaves
5 to 7 peppercorns
3 thyme sprigs
About 3 quarts cold water

. . . .

Remove the giblets from the cavity of the chicken and discard. Cut off the legs and wings, then cut the carcass in half. Place all the chicken pieces in a large pot along with the onion, celery, carrot, bay leaves, peppercorns, and thyme. Add cold water to cover; the chicken should be completely submerged.

Place the pot over high heat and bring to a boil. Decrease the heat to achieve a simmer and cook for about 1 hour, until the chicken is tender and cooked through. Periodically skim the fat and impurities off the surface during cooking. Remove the chicken from the broth and allow it to cool slightly. Shred the meat from the bones and discard the skin.

Return the bones to the pot and simmer for 1 hour to extract the rest of the flavor. Pass the broth through a fine-mesh strainer before using and discard the solids. The broth can be covered and refrigerated for 3 days or frozen for up to 6 months.

Even though vegetables are an integral part of Mexican cuisine, strictly vegetarian dishes are not as prevalent. At Doña Tomás, we consciously work in three to four dishes on each menu that either cater to vegetarians or can be altered for vegetarians. This recipe is certainly useful for those preparations.

CALDO DE VEGETALES

• VEGETABLE BROTH •
• MAKES 1 QUART •

1 white onion, chopped
2 carrots, chopped
2 celery stalks, chopped
2 bay leaves
6 peppercorns
About 1 quart cold water
Kosher salt

. . . .

Place the onion, carrots, celery, bay leaves, and peppercorns in a large pot over high heat. Cover with the water and bring to a boil. Decrease the heat to achieve a simmer and add a few pinches of salt. Cook for 20 minutes, until the flavors marry. Pass through a fine-mesh strainer, pressing any juice out of the vegetables with the back of a ladle. Discard the solids. Use at once or cover and refrigerate for up to 1 week or freeze for up to 3 months.

Many of our sauces can easily be interchanged and used for a wide number of dishes. As with all cuisines, it's important to know the basics before you practice more complicated dishes, which is why we've included this recipe for a simple tomato sauce that would typically be used in French or Italian cuisine. It serves as the foundation for a dish such as Fideo (page 83) but is also useful for many other applications.

SALSA DE TOMATE

• TOMATO SAUCE •
• MAKES 1 QUART •

8 Early Girl or vine-ripened tomatoes,
    or 10 Roma tomatoes, coarsely chopped
2 tablespoons canola oil
1 white onion, diced
1 teaspoon dried oregano
About 2 tablespoons kosher salt

. . . .

Place the tomatoes in a blender with any residual juice and purée on high speed until smooth.

Place a large skillet over high heat and add the oil. When the oil is hot, add the onion and sauté, stirring constantly, for 3 to 5 minutes, until translucent. Add the oregano and salt, and continue to sauté for 1 minute to soften the herb and bring out its flavor. Add the tomato purée and bring to a boil. Adjust the seasoning with salt as necessary.

Decrease the heat to low and simmer gently for no more than 20 minutes to gently break down the pulp of the tomatoes without ridding them of their acidity. Be sure the sauce does not boil and over-reduce; you do not want it to become too thick. Add a few tablespoons of water if necessary to adjust the consistency.

Pass the sauce through the fine plate of a food mill into a clean bowl. (Or transfer the sauce to a blender and purée on high speed for 30 seconds.) The final sauce should be thinner and more acidic than marinara, but retain a bit of body from the crushed tomatoes.

Use at once or cover and refrigerate for 2 to 3 days; we don't recommend freezing this sauce. When reheating, be careful that the sauce does not over reduce; add a few tablespoons of water to maintain the consistency.

This syrup is used in many of our sweetened drink recipes. It can be made in large or small batches, depending on your drinking habits (we only contend with very large batches so that says quite a bit about our sense of decorum). It's nice to have a batch of it available when entertaining unexpected company. The only danger to storing simple syrup is having it pick up other flavors from the refrigerator.

JARABE SIMPLE

• SIMPLE SYRUP •
• MAKES ABOUT 3 CUPS •

2 cups granulated sugar
2 cups water

....

Place the sugar and water in a small stainless steel saucepan and bring to a boil over high heat. Cook for about 2 to 3 minutes, until the sugar is completely dissolved. Remove from the heat and allow to cool. Cover and refrigerate for up to 2 weeks. As mentioned earlier, ours never lasts very long.

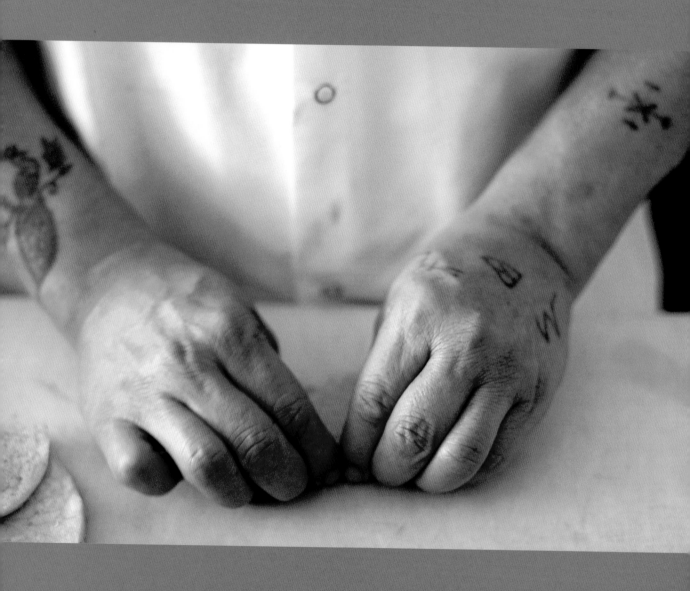

SOURCES

We recommend the following sources as starting places, but nothing is as valuable as taking a walk through your Latin American community. Linguistically challenged individuals may find it easier to ask about items in person than on the telephone. We believe that building relationships with purveyors is similar to going to the market, touching the produce, or telling the butcher what cut of meat we want—often giving rise to new ideas and bringing a sense of place to our cooking.

. . . .

LOCAL SOURCES

BAYSHORE FARMERS' MARKET

300 Bayshore Blvd.
San Francisco, CA 94124
(415) 647-1806
Fresh produce, dried peppers, and some spices.

BELMAR-LA GALLINITA MEAT MARKET

2989 24th St.
San Francisco, CA 94102
(415) 826-8880
Tripe, beef bavette, beef tongue, and other specialty cuts.

CASA LUCAS MARKET

2934 24th St.
San Francisco, CA 94102
(415) 826-4334
Specialty produce, dried peppers, spices, cheeses, and equipment.

EL CHICO PRODUCE #4

2965 Mission St.
San Francisco, CA 94110
(415) 643-4550
Specialty produce, dried peppers, spices, cheeses, meats, and crema.

EL MERCADITO MARKET

5838 International Blvd.
Oakland, CA 94621
(510) 635-3513
Fresh masa, dried chiles, Mexican spices, and equipment.

FERRY PLAZA FARMERS' MARKET

Ferry Building
San Francisco, California 94111
(415) 291-3276
Fresh and dried chiles, specialty produce, beans.

LA FINCA TORTILLERIA

3801 Foothill Blvd.
Oakland, CA 94601
(510) 536-1200
Produce, fresh masa, dried chiles, herbs, spices, and equipment.

LA PALMA MEXICATESSEN

2884 24th St.
San Francisco, CA 94110
(415) 647-1500
Fresh masa, dried peppers, spices, chorizo, *chicharrones*, *queso fresco*, crema, and equipment.

MI TIERRA FOODS
2096 San Pablo Ave.
Berkeley, CA 94702
(510) 540-6972
Chiles, masa, meats, fresh produce.

TACUBAYA
1788 4th St.
Berkeley, CA 94710
(510) 525-5160
Fresh masa, dried chiles, herbs, spices,
equipment, books, and lots of good
breakfast and lunch dishes.

OTHER RELIABLE SOURCES

BURNS FARMS
1345 Bay Lake Loop
Groveland, FL 34736
(352) 429-4048
Huitlacoche and fresh *hoja santa*.

THE CHILE GUY
168 East Calle Don Francisco
Bernalillo, NM 87004
(800) 869-9218
(505) 867-4251
Dried chiles.

MOUNTAIN MEADOWS MEAD
12 Third St.
Westwood, CA 96137
(530) 256-3233
Specialty meads.

THE MOZZARELLA COMPANY
2944 Elm St.
Dallas, TX 75226
(800) 798-2954
(214) 741-4072
www.mozzco.com
Specialty Mexican cheeses: *queso fresco,*
queso Oaxaca, hoja santa, goat cheese.

INDEX

C

FREE PUBLIC LIBRARY UNION, NEW JERSEY

3 9549 00409 7995